HOW TO GROW TREES INDOORS

HOW TO GROW TREES INDOORS

BY

Penny and Cronan Minton

Doubleday & Company, Inc.
GARDEN CITY, NEW YORK

Unless otherwise credited, all photographs were taken by Cronan Minton.

Acknowledgments

The help and kindness of dozens of people made researching and writing this book a pleasant and fascinating task. For their editorial suggestions, information, patience, and encouragement, we would especially like to thank Mr. and Mrs. Martin McShane of Wildwood Gardens, North Conway, N.H. And we are equally as indebted to Mr. Fred Hager, supervisor of the greenhouse for indoor trees at John's "Dewkist" Nurseries, Apopka, Fla.

Mrs. Juel Sheffield and her assistant Mr. Mike Purdy at Plants 'N Things, Roanoke, Va., spent hours talking to us and kindly let us photograph many of their indoor trees. Other nurserymen who helped were Mr. C. A. Alford, Gurney Gardens, Roanoke, Va.; Mr. Joseph G. Meola, Nielsen's Garden Center, Darien, Conn.; and the people at The Plant Shack, Roanoke, Va.

Invaluable advice came from Dr. Charles A. Conover, Center Director, Agricultural Research Center, Apopka, Fla.; Dr. James Crow, U. S. Botanic Garden, Washington, D.C.; Larry Durky, Green Thumb, Inc., Apopka, Fla.; Dr. Richard S. Lindstrom, Virginia Polytechnic Institute, Blacksburg, Va., and Mr. and Mrs. Richard Rogers, Apopka, Fla. Special thanks for photographic assistance are due to Ms. Monica Daley, Salem, Va.; Mr. L. B. Bailey, Williamson Road Photo Shop, Roanoke, Va.; William Rand, Fincastle, Va.; and Mr. and Mrs. Robert W. Minton, Concord, Mass.

For library assistance we are grateful to Mr. Michael Mayo, Roanoke County Public Library, Hollins Branch, Hollins, Va.

We would also like to thank our agent, Max Gartenberg, for suggesting the idea, and our editor at Doubleday, Karen Van Westering, for helping us to see it through.

Equally as deserving of thanks are Mrs. Hulda Bridgeman, Roanoke, Va.; Mrs. Wisey Bullington, New Orleans, La.; Mr. Daniel Lavezzo III, New York, N.Y.; Mrs. D. H. Patterson-Knight, McLean, Va.; and Mr. Rudy Custer, Business Manager of the Chicago Bears football club, for his enthusiastic advice on growing citrus trees indoors.

Last but not least, we appreciate the loan of photographs from Debby Sempsrott, Everett Conklin Companies, Montvale, N.J., and from Mr. Kenneth Magistrate and Mr. Richard Champion, Terrestris, New York.

Contents

Appendix

Introduction

We can remember a spectacular modern house in the town where we grew up which had a tree growing in the living room. To us this seemed like the height of luxury. The tree grew on a small island in the middle of a blue-tiled pool. The water was filled with scarlet goldfish. It would never have occurred to us that we would one day have trees growing in our own house, or that thousands of other people would have indoor trees as well. But today indoor trees are everywhere. They are as available in tropical plant stores as African violets and Boston ferns. And they are adding a dramatic new look to the interiors of countless American homes.

Indoor trees are also appearing more and more frequently in public buildings. Store fronts in New York City are filled with indoor trees. In almost any modern shopping mall, you can find magnificent scheffleras growing twenty feet high or more, palms and oddly shaped marginatas, ficuses of numerous varieties, along with corn plants, dumb canes, ming trees, yucca trees, not to mention bamboo.

In short, the wonderful thing about indoor trees today is their tremendous variety and the fact that you can buy them fully grown. You don't have to wait five or ten years to grow them yourself. And sometimes for as little as $15 or $20 you can buy a four- or five-foot tree.

But many indoor gardeners have also become fascinated by the challenge of trying to grow small plants into trees. A friend from Chicago writes us passionate letters about the progress of his citrus trees. One of his grapefruit trees is eight feet tall and has been growing in his living room for twenty years. He grew this tree and others like it strictly from seed. Other people are equally as devoted to growing avocado trees. One can also buy seedling tropical trees for a dollar or two, or bushy foliage plants for under $10, and grow them into trees. Plants such as *Schefflera,* rubber plant, dumb cane, *Fatsia japonica,* and silk oak can grow over a foot a year with proper care. On the other hand, mature trees are so instantly dramatic that they are worth the extra cost in terms of what they can do to enhance a room.

Some friends of ours own a unique modern house with a thirty-foot ceiling in their living room. The room is dominated by a soaring twenty-foot yucca tree and a ten-foot saguaro cactus. The only other plants in the room are a bushy citrus and a large gardenia, which blooms perpetually because the room is just about all glass. The two small plants add a colorful touch, but without the yucca and the tall cactus tree to take up all that space, the room might look overwhelmingly tall. Besides, the yucca tree is a fantastic conversation piece. Instead of running for the liquor, awkward guests can stand around the tree and gawk.

Plants of all shapes and sizes are wonderful to have around the home, and we have no desire to argue that tree-size houseplants are superior to plants in small pots. Our house is filled with miniature palms, dracaenas, cactuses, and ferns in hanging baskets, as well as taller trees. In fact, we probably pay more attention to our plants when they are young than we do when they become tall. By then we feel we've done our work. Half the fun of having plants, after all, is watching them *grow*. But the main advantage of an indoor tree is that it fills up empty space and adds both lushness and dramatic impact to a room. Two or three large plants can create the same effect as thirty or forty small ones.

The Purpose of This Book

With correct watering and an adequate amount of light, anyone can grow an indoor tree. But it can be frustrating at first—not to mention costly—unless you know something about the growth habits of your tree.

Indoor trees often need different care than smaller plants, especially when it comes to water and light. It is easy enough to fit a small plant on a window sill if it needs strong light, but what do you do with a six- or seven-foot tree? How often should you water a tree in a large pot? Surprisingly, trees in large containers require *less* frequent watering than small plants in small pots.

Since indoor trees are such a relatively new phenomenon, information about them is still scarce. Some species are discussed as *plants* in books on indoor gardening, but no book has yet been written for the general reader which groups all the indoor trees under one cover and discusses their growing requirements in detail. This is where we hope our book can help you out.

Our research has taken us through greenhouses and plant stores from Florida to Maine, and we have tracked down as many species of indoor trees as we could find. Some, like the mahogany tree, proved to be so rare that we decided to exclude them from the book. Others, such as tree geraniums and gardenias, did not strike us as sufficiently tree-like to qualify as indoor trees. In some cases, emotional attachment to a particular kind of plant influenced our decision to call it a tree. The Jerusalem cherry, for instance, does not grow very tall, but it has a woody trunk and we love it for its resemblance to a tree. The jade plant also falls under this category.

We have written separate essays—arranged in alphabetical order by the trees' most commonly used names—on all the indoor trees that can be found in plant stores today. Not all of them are easy to find, or easy to grow, but the majority of them are. We have also made each essay long enough so that you won't have to refer back to the introductory chapters on general care if you are pressed for time. But we urge you to read these chapters first to familiarize yourself with what all indoor trees basically need. The chapters on watering, lighting, and containers are especially important, and other topics can be read as specific questions or problems arise.

Our Own Experience with Indoor Trees

Thirteen years ago, when we first got married, we knew absolutely nothing about indoor trees. In fact, we knew absolutely nothing about plants. One of us (Penny) had tried to grow a rubber tree once, but that experiment failed dismally.

If we had only known about indoor trees, we might have avoided the typical problem faced by newlyweds of how to make an apartment or a house feel like a home. All we had when we moved into our first apartment was a convertible couch, a table, and two chairs—all purchased second-hand—and heaps of superfluous wedding gifts such as silver ash trays, cigarette cases, crystal salt shakers, and silver nut bowls. We also had duplicates of things such as electric frying pans, electric popcorn poppers, electric coffeepots, and electric toasters—most of which we eventually gave away as wedding gifts to our friends.

But our apartment was bare. We were living in a wing of a converted mental hospital hastily erected during World War II. There were exposed pipes and fire sprinklers in the ceiling. When we flushed the toilet, the reverberation shook the living room. We may have bought one or two small cactuses, but for the most part we used hedge clippings in place of plants and cut flowers that we bought once a week for a dollar a bunch.

Today, much of the hideousness of that apartment could be camouflaged with indoor trees. A schefflera could be stationed in one corner, a corn plant or a *Dracaena marginata* in another, hanging baskets hung in the windows, and smaller plants placed around the room for accent. But those apartments are past history now and will never house an indoor tree.

Our first real acquaintance with indoor gardening did not come until several years later, when we moved to Washington, D.C. A major riot erupted that fall following the assassination of Martin Luther King, Jr.

From our living room, we could see the skyline in flames. Down in the street, a variety of mad things was going on. National guardsmen stood sentry at street corners and fire trucks screamed by. Our apartment was located right beside a fire station and right above a Chinese restaurant. Night and day, we were overwhelmed by the smell of Chinese cooking and the crisis atmosphere created by the sirens. Our enormous landlady roamed the halls at night, brandishing a .45.

One day in winter, after the riots had passed, one of us brought home a small green rubber tree. The next week we added a philodendron and a small palm. Gradually, we began collecting plants.

Although we did not realize it then, we were obviously responding to the tensions of city life by trying to create a livable environment indoors. In 1968, we moved to an apartment located in an even grimmer section of the city. In 1969, we fled. But occasionally there were moments of peace, moments of delight, when we would notice a new leaf unfolding from the philodendron, or a moment of despair when our rubber tree dropped another leaf.

Indoor trees entered our lives once and for all in 1971, when we moved south to the Roanoke Valley in the Blue Ridge Mountains of Virginia. There we lived in a house on two lush acres, beautifully landscaped with apple, pear, plum, cherry, quince, and persimmon trees, as well as dogwoods, maples, locusts, and pines.

Our fascination with indoor trees really began in an environment that was harmonious to growth. It was as if the trees outside inspired us to grow trees and plants inside. When a discount store that carried indoor trees went bankrupt, we descended on it and brought home a tall *Dracaena marginata,* a loquat, two scheffleras, a rubber tree, and several palms.

And we were on our way. Our house became a jungle of tropical growth. We grew tomatoes, lettuce, and corn outside in the summer, and in the fall and winter we concentrated on our indoor trees. Our marginata grew a foot a year. One of our scheffleras grew faster than that. Visitors expressed amazement at all the growth. The atmosphere was so fecund that ivy on the brick wall outside worked its way through a crack in a window frame and invaded our living room. Along with trees and ferns in hanging baskets, we suddenly had great strands of ivy cascading to the floor. We became passionate growers of all sorts of things.

And so we would like to open up this world to you. Houseplants are marvelous. But the crown of creation when it comes to indoor gardening is the "big stuff"— large, lush, beautiful indoor trees.

Part I

Secrets to Better Growth For Your Indoor Trees

How to Grow a
Houseplant into a Tree

Unlike Jack's magical beanstalk, houseplants do not spring into trees overnight. It takes patience to grow an indoor tree, but thousands of people have done it, and so can you. There are fast-growing trees such as the schefflera which can put on a foot of new growth a year (and sometimes more) in the right environment and with proper care. Other trees are so slow-growing that they never seem to budge an inch.

On the other hand, if you can afford to buy a full-grown indoor tree, you will happily discover that many such plants are hardier and easier to care for than younger and more tender plants. Their size and age indicate that they have survived the hazards of infancy and childhood, at least. Their root systems are exten-

The trees in these photos are both *Pleomele reflexa*. The one on the left is a medium-sized plant that has not been pruned or shaped. The tree on the right shows the elegant tree-like shape this plant can attain with proper attention.

sive and well established. They are used to living in containers. *They rarely need watering more than once a week, fertilizing more than twice a year, and repotting more than once every five years.* And if you keep them pruned, they will not outgrow your home.

The only stumbling blocks that mature indoor trees must initially overcome are the lighting and atmospheric conditions of your home—and you, the new grower. It may take both of you a while to get accustomed to each other's habits.

Since mature indoor trees cost anywhere from $15 to $100, and usually average between $30 and $40, you will naturally want to treat your investment with care. The period of transition from the hothouse or the plant shop to your home is critical for certain species (weeping fig, Indian laurel, citrus, Norfolk Island pine, pittosporum, privet, and sago palm, to name a few). If your new tree weathers the first two or three months without harm, it should cause you little or no trouble from then on.

To ensure that this transition period is successful, we urge you to read the chapters on water and light, as well as the essay on your particular tree. Correct watering and proper lighting will virtually guarantee that your tree will live a long, long time. The size of the tree does not mean that it is old (most indoor trees in plant shops are under five years old), and it should survive for five, ten, or even twenty years if you continue to give it proper care.

If you are ambitious to grow an ordinary houseplant into a tree, you will meet with less frustration if you choose a fast-growing species and adhere to a few simple growing rules. We can't promise miracles, and we reiterate the need for patience. It takes anywhere from two to ten years to grow a houseplant into a tree, depending on the species and the care you give to it. Learn to practice the art of looking away, of seeming not to care, the grace of nonchalance. If you accept the fact that nature, when confined to the indoors, can't compete with General Motors or Ford, you will wake up one fine morning and realize that your plant has suddenly begun to look like a tree.

Some of the fastest-growing indoor trees are:

> Dumb cane
> False aralia
> *Fatsia japonica*
> Rubber tree
> Schefflera
> Silk oak
> Tree philodendron

These are all fairly conventional tropical plants which can be found in almost any plant store.

Other plants to consider are:

> Avocado
> Banana
> *Dracaena marginata*
> *Dracaena warnecki*
> Eucalyptus
> Fiddle-leaf fig
> Indian laurel

Jerusalem cherry
Pencil cactus
Poinsettia
Weeping fig

Our most satisfying results have come from scheffleras, rubber trees, philodendrons, Jerusalem cherry trees, and *Dracaena marginata*. Friends of ours have had great success with dumb canes, silk oaks, and false aralias. Avocado plants grow fast, but they rarely make good-looking trees. Banana and eucalyptus are sometimes difficult to grow. The *Dracaena marginata* is often labeled as a slow-growing tree, but one of ours has grown nearly a foot a year for the last three years (although most marginatas average four to six inches a year). The Jerusalem cherry does not grow into a tall tree, but it puts on a wondrous amount of new growth every year. The weeping fig and the Indian laurel will grow as much as a foot a year indoors with proper care. The poinsettia grows like a weed in summer, but you may not like its looks as it matures, since it develops a skinny stem.

The magical beans that poor Jack traded his skinny cow for, and that his mother subsequently whipped him for and threw out the window of their ramshackle house, grew unbelievably by the light of the full moon. However, do not expect moonlight to add more than a billionth of an inch of new growth a year to the height of your trees. The essential ingredient for rapid growth is sunlight—strong,

This is a striking example of the different rates at which plants grow and truly become trees. The large schefflera grew six feet high from seed in less than two years. The small yew pine (*Podocarpus*) in the foreground grew only six inches in the same length of time.

rich, warm, brilliant sunlight. Keeping plants outdoors in spring, summer, and early fall also helps. For best results, keep the following general suggestions in mind:

Light—Keep the plant (or plants) in the brightest location in your home. Rooms with southern or eastern exposures are the brightest. Light-colored walls increase light intensity. So do clean windows without curtains. Use 150-watt, incandescent spotlights or fluorescent lights for five or six hours at night in fall and winter to supplement natural light if necessary.

Water—Never increase watering to speed up the growth of a plant. Always allow the surface of the soil to dry out before drenching the container.

Fertilizing—Use a timed-release or water-soluble fertilizer according to instructions on the label. Timed-release fertilizers provide more constant and even feeding than water-soluble fertilizers, which lose their effectiveness with repeated waterings. Never overfertilize.

Repotting—Repot plants with commercial potting soil, and step up the size of the pot by one or two inches. Do this every one to three years depending on how fast the plant is growing. Do not repot mature trees more than once every five years.

Fresh air—Put plants outside or on a screened-in porch in spring, summer, and early fall. Do not expose them to full sunlight for the first two weeks. Then only give full sun to species that will tolerate it. Be on the alert for an increase in bugs, and hose the leaves down early in the morning or at sunset to keep them clean. Watch out for high winds and storms. Also watch for moldy soil and funguses. Open windows and doors in warm weather to give plants growing indoors fresh air.

Humidity—Mist plants daily in winter, group them near other plants, and use a humidifier if you have one.

Pruning—Pruning stimulates fuller growth and is essential on young rubber plants, fiddle-leaf figs, coffee trees, Jerusalem cherry trees, avocado plants, and poinsettias. Prune these species at least once a year in spring. Clip one to two inches off the top of stems and branches, just above where a leaf or leaves join the stem. Prune other species to encourage symmetrical growth.

Easy and Difficult Trees to Grow Indoors

As a general rule, tropical trees with soft, succulent stems such as the schefflera and *Dracaena marginata* are easier to grow indoors than woody species from subtropical and temperate regions such as citrus trees, privet, yew pine, *Pittosporum*, and loquat. The latter usually require a dormant period in winter and need cool air and good air circulation to look their best from year to year. They also need extremely bright light.

Another consideration is how certain species look indoors as they mature. Coffee plants are beautiful when young, but it is difficult to grow a handsome coffee *tree*. Avocado plants are entertaining, but avocado trees can be a pain. Both species need frequent pruning when young to look attractive as they grow into trees. But pruning them may not even do much good. Their leaves grow farther and farther apart, dry out easily, and often get crinkly and brown.

The same holds true for the banana tree, which looks gorgeous as a young green plant, but which often looks horrendous as it develops into a tree (even in nature its leaves become brown at the edges and ragged). The silk oak (*Grevillea robusta*) is fairly attractive as a plant, but it grows so fast and gets so tall and skinny that within a few short years it can look like a silly weed. The loquat tree and the fiddle-leaf fig are also difficult to manage.

If any one of these trees ends up disappointing you, it is not necessarily your fault. They all have bad track records as indoor trees.

The following is a list of easy, moderately easy to difficult, and just plain ornery trees to grow indoors. By "easy," we mean most hardy and least demanding. "Moderate" may present problems at times. "Difficult" trees require ideal growing conditions to look their best.

EASY	MODERATE	DIFFICULT
Candelabra cactus	Areca palm	Autograph tree
Corn plant, *Dracaena fragrans*	Avocado	Banana
Dracaena warnecki	Bamboo palm	Citrus
Dumb cane	Coffee tree	Croton
Jade	Coral berry	Eucalyptus
Jerusalem cherry	False aralia	Jasmine
Kentia palm	Fan palm	Loquat
Ming tree	Fishtail palm	Privet
Pencil cactus	Hawaiian ti	Sea grape
Philodendron	Indian laurel	Tree ferns
Pleomela	Lady palm	
Ponytail palm	Parlor palm	
Rubber tree	Pittosporum	
Schefflera	Poinsettia	
Screw pine	Sago palm	
Yucca	Silk oak	
	Weeping fig	
	Yew pine	

Please do not take this list as gospel truth. You may have wonderful success growing some of the "difficult" trees and terrible luck with some of the "easy" ones. It all depends on where you live, what kind of light your home receives, how you set your thermostat, and whether you water the trees correctly and give them good general care. An experienced indoor gardener should be able to grow all these trees with a fair amount of success.

Growing Trees from Your Own Back Yard Indoors

We approach this subject with trepidation and extreme humility. We have never grown a temperate tree indoors in our life. Moreover, in the course of writing this book, we could find no professionals or amateurs who had tried it either.

But, obviously, trees such as maple, oak, birch, and pine are infinitely more difficult to keep alive indoors than tropical species. They all need extremely bright light, high humidity, fresh air, and cool air in winter to survive. Few if any people ever try to grow such trees indoors, because most temperate trees lose their leaves in winter. As a result, they are of little value as decorative trees during the fall and winter months.

However, several horticulturists expressed an interest in the subject to us, and they also gave us some suggestions on how such trees *might* be grown indoors.

First, all temperate trees need a dormant period in winter to survive. Specifically, they need 2,000 to 2,500 hours of dormancy, meaning two or three months. This would involve moving a temperate tree to a very cool location between 35 and 45 degrees (or putting it outside in a cold frame) and keeping it out of range of electric lights at night. Watering would have to be reduced to once a month or less and no fertilizer added to the soil from September or October until February or March.

If such a tree were placed in cold storage October 1 and went through its normal process of defoliation, it could theoretically be brought back into a warm room in early January. To force it to bud and grow new leaves before spring, keep it in the brightest window in your home and supplement its light with five or six hours of strong artificial lighting at night. Water moderately at first (about once every two or three weeks) until the tree shows signs of life. Then begin to water it more regularly and apply fertilizer (half the recommended strength) to the soil. Mist the young leaves every day.

One sure sign that temperate trees are difficult to grow indoors is that most species of bonsai trees are temperate, and these are always kept outdoors except on special occasions when they are brought inside for a day or two. This applies especially to pine trees, which need cool air in winter, good air circulation, high humidity, and bright light. The only way that you could keep a pine alive indoors would be to put it on an unheated sun porch and mist its needles often and throw open the windows during the day. If the Chinese and Japanese have been growing bonsai trees outdoors for the last ten centuries, it figures that they must know what they're doing.

The only suggestion we can offer is, give temperate trees a try and see how they work. It doesn't cost a penny to dig a seedling up, and no money will be lost if the tree dies, although the failure may hurt your pride. Theoretically, the best seedlings to use would be ones that have been growing in gloom on the forest floor. These might adapt a little easier to reduced light in your home.

You might also be curious to try growing an acorn or a chestnut or various kinds of fruit seeds such as apple, pear, plum, and peach. It will take godlike patience, since such seeds take a long time to germinate. There is a method of growing seeds known as *stratification* which will work best with the seeds of fruit trees. This involves sowing the seeds in a pot filled with potting soil, covering them over lightly with soil, then putting them outdoors for two or three months during the winter to be frozen and thawed, snowed upon, rained upon, and dried out. In March, bring the pot back inside and keep it moist and in a bright location out of direct sunlight. Seedlings will begin to appear slowly over the course of several months.

Soil

It is neither wise nor in the long run economical to use ordinary garden soil when repotting indoor trees. You simply increase the risk of losing the tree. Commercial potting soil may strike you as expensive, but it is blatantly the better growing medium to use.

One of the troubles with ordinary garden soil is that it dries out like cement. Another problem is that it is crawling with germs and bugs. But its worst feature is that it packs too tightly into the bottom of pots. It traps stagnant water down there which can cut off the supply of oxygen to the roots of a plant and make them rot. This is why gravel or clay shards were always used in the bottom of pots, to ensure adequate drainage for soil that otherwise might clog the drainage hole.

Now—and this may come as a surprise to you—gravel and clay shards are not really necessary if you pot your trees with commercially prepared soil. No matter what brand you use, these soils are lighter and more porous and do not clog drainage holes. Moreover, the lightness of the soil enables roots to move around more freely and breathe more air, both of which make for a healtheir root system and a faster-growing tree.

Commercial soils hold water longer, too.

There was a time when indoor gardeners used loam, leaf mold, manure, peat moss, compost, and mixed up special batches of homemade soil. But today fewer and fewer people have access to such soils. Imagine digging up a bucket full of dirt in Central Park. And what about manure? You would have to run along behind a mounted policeman waiting for his horse to perform.

Packaged potting soils consist either of peat moss with perlite or vermiculite mixed in (along with a sprinkling of superphosphates and lime) or of peat moss and sterilized loam. The former is preferred by many professional growers, but the latter is often less expensive and is the kind we use. The peat-loam mixture looks more like real dirt. The peat-vermiculite mixture is often so dry and powdery it looks more like moon dust. It doesn't really matter which kind of mixture you use. But do not be deceived by all the fancy labels reading "cactus soil," "philodendron soil," "azalea soil," etc. *Ordinary potting soil is excellent for all species of indoor trees.* Sand can be added to soils for succulents and cactuses if you like (although there is no real need to do this), and acid fertilizer can be fed to azaleas and philodendrons. We have several huge philodendrons and have always grown them in ordinary potting soil, and used ordinary fertilizer on them, too. It is just a waste of money buying different kinds of soils for different trees and plants. A special "cactus soil" is different from ordinary potting soil only in that it contains more sand. "Azalea soil" is slightly more acidic. On the whole, these special soils are designed to tempt the gullible into buying more soil.

When shopping for potting soil, inspect the fine print on the bag to determine its *volume* instead of its weight. The label (usually near the bottom of the bag) will list the weight (five, ten, or twenty pounds) and also the volume (five, ten, or twenty quarts). An element of deception creeps in when it comes to buying by weight, since many companies add water to their soil to increase its weight. You may think that you are getting a bargain on a "ten-pound" bag, when in fact a five-pound bag might have just the same volume and cost less. So when you compare the price on two different brands of soil, compare their volumes, too. We usually buy large, twenty-pound bags of potting soil at the hardware store or local discount store for under $4 (the bag contains twenty quarts of soil, and this *is* a good deal). If you are repotting indoor trees, you will need to buy your soil in a quantity at least as great as this.

Mixing Your Own Soil

In spite of the fact that packaged potting soil is widely available, some people still enjoy mixing their own soil. The result may not necessarily be a better grade of soil, but it can be less expensive, and it also brings one closer to the growing process as a whole.

One reliable and simple formula for mixing soil is to combine peat moss and perlite (or vermiculite) in a ratio of 60 per cent peat moss to 40 per cent perlite or vermiculite. Peat moss can be purchased inexpensively by the bag or bale at most discount stores which have a garden center. If they don't have perlite or vermiculite, you can find either of these in most plant stores. Perlite is a fluffy volcanic glass with a high water-holding capacity; vermiculite is a form of ground-up mica with a moisture capacity equally as high. If the peat moss-perlite mixture strikes you as too fluffy, you can add sand to give it weight. The formula should then read (roughly): 20 per cent sand, 40 per cent peat moss, and 40 per cent perlite or vermiculite.

A truly experienced indoor gardener who has mixed his own soil for years would then add crushed limestone, organic bone meal, and/or superphosphates to the soil. The limestone would counteract the acidity of the peat moss, and the bone meal or superphosphates would act as fertilizer. *But we urge you not to use these ingredients unless you really know what you are doing.* It is much easier and safer to use an ordinary water-soluble fertilizer or a timed-release fertilizer, and forget about the limestone altogether. If you make a large batch of soil which you plan to store for future use, do not mix the fertilizer in with the whole batch. Fertilize each tree or plant *individually* after the new soil has been added, and follow fertilizing instructions on the package.

A more organic formula for mixing soil consists of 60 per cent compost combined with 40 per cent perlite or vermiculite (or 20 per cent sand, 40 per cent compost and 40 per cent perlite or vermiculite). But be sure the compost is fully decomposed (preferably a year old). Raw compost that is still decomposing will burn the roots of an indoor tree or plant. It is not necessary to sterilize compost by baking it, since the sterilizing process has already taken place in the inferno of the compost heap. Fertilize the compost-perlite mixture the same way as above.

The least desirable formula for homemade potting soil consists of 60 per cent garden soil and 40 per cent perlite or vermiculite. The garden soil should be baked in an oven at 350 degrees for an hour or more to kill germs and weeds. Then mix it with the perlite or vermiculite. We have already mentioned why garden soil is basically taboo for potted trees and plants: it packs too tightly in the pot and dries out much too fast. Moreover, the baking process is laborious and messy. And who wants dirt mixed in with their meat loaf, anyway?

Repotting

Do not be overly anxious to repot an indoor tree. Repotting is more necessary for young foliage plants than it is for mature trees. If you have invested $50 or $100 for a six-to-ten-foot tree, wait at least five years before you even *think* about repotting it. If the tree is doing well, don't touch it. Accidents can happen when you are repotting any plant, so there is no sense tampering with the tree if all is going well. As we mention later (in the essay on the Norfolk Island pine) one woman we know grew her tree in the same container for twenty years. She never once removed it from its pot or changed its soil!

Knowing when to repot an indoor tree is largely a matter of instinct. After one of our younger trees has been in the same container for several years (anywhere from two to five), we get a feeling one fine day that the tree has not grown much lately and that it needs a larger container and fresh soil. A tree that needs repotting will let you know, since its growth will noticeably slow down. It may also become a glutton for water. The best idea is to keep an eye on it in spring. If new leaves are smaller and scarcer than they were the spring before, and if by July nothing much has happened, the tree most likely needs repotting. The only other problem it could be is lack of fertilizer or lack of light. We may put off repotting the tree for a week or several months depending on our energy. Then, on a sunny day when we have nothing else to do, we will move the tree outside and get to work. Inevitably, other of our plants and trees come outside with us as well.

There is something immensely satisfying about repotting once we get around to it. The entire process, from the moment we open up the bag of soil and see the rich damp earth inside, to shaking the tree loose from its pot and seeing all of its imprisoned and dried-out roots, is fascinating. We feel as if we are liberating the tree, giving it a new lease on life. Mentally, we say, "Here we are, tree. Sorry we waited so long to change your soil. It's really amazing that you could stand living so long in this cramped pot. Wait until you see how good you feel in this new soil."

To be frank, our feelings about liberation and renewal may apply more to ourselves than to the tree. They may be totally romantic and subjective and have nothing to do with the tree's real needs. There are horticulturists who argue that repotting is superfluous, that potting soil does not exhaust itself so long as it is fertilized. This may well be true for specimen-size trees (trees, that is, which look just right the way they are, which you would not want to grow any larger), but a young tree that is still growing will need a larger pot to expand.

The new container should be one to two inches larger than the old one; it is pointless and even dangerous to increase the size of the pot by more than two inches. If the tree is already in a container twelve or thirteen inches in diameter, it does *not* need a larger pot. However, if growth has come to a standstill, the tree may need to have its roots trimmed (see root trimming discussion below).

When repotting an indoor tree, wait until the old soil in the pot is moderately dry. Otherwise you will have a mess on your hands. Remove the tree by shaking it back and forth to loosen the soil. If the tree is really tenacious, loosen the soil by carefully sliding a knife around the insides of the pot, as if you were removing a cake from a pan. To prevent root damage, *do not shake the old soil loose from the roots*. Lay the tree carefully on its side, prop it up against a wall, or have someone hold it up for you. Place fresh potting soil in the bottom of the new container. If some of the roots hanging from the root ball look damaged or rotten, clip them off with a pair of clean scissors. Then slide the root ball gently into the new container and pour fresh potting soil around the sides. Keep on adding soil and packing it gently around the roots until the soil comes up above the level of the topmost roots. Pack the soil down firmly to hold the tree in place to keep it erect. For a tall tree with a slender trunk, you may need to slide a stake into the soil at this point to keep the tree from tipping over. Now water the soil thoroughly, then wait about a week before you water it again. Do not fertilize fresh, store-bought potting soil for the first five or six months.

Root Trimming

Since extremely large pots (fourteen inches in diameter or over) are woefully heavy and hard to move around, it is more convenient to keep indoor trees confined to pots of twelve to thirteen inches in diameter. You can keep a large tree healthy in a pot this size virtually forever. If repotting seems necessary, the best thing to do is to trim the roots of the tree and replant it in the same pot or in a new pot the same size.

Root trimming can be done in two ways.

One method is to shave two inches off the *bottom* of the root ball. Use either a carving knife with a serrated blade or (radical as this may sound) a saw. Lay the tree on its side. Do not shake the old soil loose from the roots. Now saw a slice two inches wide off the bottom of the root ball. If you plan to use the same container, wash it out thoroughly first. Then fill the bottom with fresh potting soil and slide the root ball back into the pot. Fill the rest of the pot with soil as described above.

The other method is to slice one inch off *two sides* of the root ball. Imagine the root ball as a cube, and now imagine slicing one inch off two opposite sides of the cube. Hold the tree upright and saw off a slice one inch straight down one side of the root ball. Then saw off another slice the same width from the *opposite* side of the root ball. Then replant the tree as described above.

The purpose of root trimming is to decrease the size of the root ball slightly so that fresh soil can be added to the container and the roots will have new space in which to grow. The result is the same as if you had increased the size of the pot by two inches.

Root trimming will not damage an indoor tree so long as you are careful and do not treat the root ball roughly.

Containers

Trees grown in plastic containers may offend some people's sense of taste, but there is no truth to the rumor that clay pots are healthier for plants than pots made out of plastic. The soil in a clay pot dries out faster than the soil in a plastic pot. For this reason clay pots are safer to use if you are just beginning to learn how to grow trees and plants indoors. There is less chance of overwatering a tree in a clay pot and possibly killing it.

We have two small coffee plants growing on a shelf in our kitchen window. The only difference between them is their pots. One is in a red clay pot. The other is in a green plastic pot. We water the plant in the clay pot two or three times a week. But we only water the plant in the plastic pot once a week. Sometimes we only water it every nine or ten days.

This is because clay is porous and plastic is not. Water evaporates out the sides of a clay pot two or three times faster than out the topsoil of a plastic pot. People who love to water plants should really use clay pots. An indoor tree in a large plastic pot (ten inches in diameter or larger) will need water only twice a month or less, whereas a clay container the same size will most likely need water at least once a week.

There is a wealth of large containers on the market. It also takes considerable wealth to afford some of them. Along with containers made of plastic and clay you will find wooden tubs, chrome and stainless steel urns, wine casks and kegs sawed in half, and glazed terra-cotta pots. Soil in wooden containers dries out about as fast as soil in unglazed clay pots. But soil in steel containers or glazed ceramic pots takes as long to dry out as soil in plastic pots. Some of these containers do not have drainage holes. Contrary to popular opinion there is nothing wrong with this. They are perfectly usable if you realize that the soil in them takes longer to dry out than soil in containers *with* drainage holes. There is no need to take them to a glazier, as some authors suggest, and have their bottoms drilled full of holes. But be extra careful not to water them as frequently as containers with drainage holes. Always wait until the top one inch of the soil is powder-dry.

When choosing a large container, avoid flimsy ones that may split or crack if the tree in it becomes root-bound. But also consider weight. If the container is unusually heavy, just think how immovable it will be once you fill it with soil and a tree. Settle for something durable but fairly light in case you want to move the tree around. Some indoor treees are so large that they require containers filled with forty pounds of soil or more. In this case you may need to buy a dolly or to make your own with a thick piece of plywood and casters. The easiest containers to move around on casters are the box-type wooden ones.

But don't go overboard on the size of the container. Few indoor trees need pots larger than twelve or thirteen inches in diameter. When repotting a young tree that is still growing, step up the size of the container by one inch. With a tree that is already in a container twelve inches in diameter or more, you need not increase the size of the pot when repotting. Trim one to two inches off the bottom or the sides of the root ball (see page 24) and repot the tree in the same container with fresh potting soil.

Avoid spending $20 or $30 on a large container unless you find one that you really love. Take your time and shop around. Go to yard sales. You may stumble on an old milk can or an earthenware jar far back in the cobwebs of someone's garage. A flea market at a drive-in theater may have just the pot you're looking for. If you are handy with tools, build your own container out of wood. For smaller trees, consider using an inexpensive wastebasket and covering it with Con-Tact paper or repainting it and trimming it with your own designs.

One of our trees is in a large bucket that once contained roofing tar. Several others are in gallon paint cans which we conceal by placing them in baskets. We bought a hideous tulip-shaped plastic wastebasket for $.99 at a supermarket, clipped off the rim which rose and fell like tulip petals, and now as a container for a schefflera it doesn't look half bad. After all, containers for indoor trees usually stand on the floor, and if they are not particularly attractive you can always hide them behind a table, couch, or corner chair. A beautiful container admittedly makes a difference in a room, but considering how much such beauty costs, you may just have to compromise.

One of our friends has an eight-foot rubber tree growing in an old Victorian bathtub which she filled with soil and painted silver. In its own unique and offbeat way the bathtub looks fantastic. Another friend with a more rigid sense of form built a large brick planter, three feet deep by ten feet long, at one end of his living room. He lined it with tin, filled the base with gravel, added soil, and now it contains all sorts of tropical trees.

When starting new trees from clippings or seeds, save money by using old tin cans or plastic gallon milk or bleach jugs cut in half.

It does not really matter what kind of a container you use for indoor trees so long as you learn to water the soil in them correctly. All you need to remember is that porous containers made of clay and wood dry out two or three times faster than containers made of plastic, steel, or glazed clay.

Water

No aspect of growing trees indoors is more important than learning how to water them correctly. More trees probably die from overwatering than from lack of light, underwatering, low humidity, drafts, diseases, and pests combined. Unfortunately, it may be more satisfying to you to water a tree every day than it is every other week. But this is an instinct you must learn to control. It takes iron self-restraint to learn how to water indoor trees. If you read only one page or one paragraph in this section, please make it this page and the paragraph below.

The key to watering an indoor tree correctly lies in soaking the whole container and then waiting anywhere from a week to a month until the top of the soil dries out. We cannot emphasize this point too strongly. The soil must be given this period of partial drying out in order for the roots of the tree to breathe. If the soil is constantly soggy, the delicate root hairs which conduct water, oxygen, and nutrients to the tree will rot. Without root hairs, a tree cannot survive. In short, oxygen is just as important to the roots of a tree as water is, and you should be just as worried about letting them breathe as you are about giving them enough to drink.

Before you are tempted to water an indoor tree, you should first be able to pick up enough dry surface soil to sift through your fingers like dry sand. If the surface of the soil feels even slightly moist, wrestle your watering arm to the ground. Wait a few more days and check the soil again. Scratch down through the top inch of the soil to see how it looks and feels. Is it dark and damp, or is it dry and crumbly? If the latter, you can now water the tree.

With water-loving trees such as palms and tree ferns, water the soil as soon as the surface dries out. But with most species wait until the top one to two inches of the soil are powder-dry.

If you follow these instructions, you will soon discover that indoor trees require far *less* frequent watering than small plants in small pots. The more soil a pot contains, the more water it will hold and the longer the soil will take to dry out. Where a small plant in a small pot may need water every other day, an indoor tree in a large container may need water only once every two weeks or as seldom as once a month. It all depends on how large the pot is, whether it is plastic or clay, what kind of soil the pot contains, and what the season is. Soil in clay pots dries out at least twice as fast as soil in plastic pots. Pots with drainage holes dry out faster than pots without drainage holes. Ordinary garden loam dries out faster than commercial potting soil. Soil dries out faster in spring and summer than it does in fall and winter. Try to think of each of your trees as individuals with different needs, and water them accordingly. It is unlikely that they will all need water at the same time.

When watering, don't be miserly. Give the pot a good, thorough soaking. Make sure all the soil gets moist. Add enough water so that water begins pouring out the drainage holes. Then empty the dish in which the pot stands.

We pour about a half gallon of water in pots ten to twelve inches in diameter. Containers from thirteen to seventeen inches need anywhere from three fourths of a gallon of water to two or three gallons. In other words, do not go around watering indoor trees with a delicate little watering can. Use a large container such as a plastic gallon milk jug or buy a five gallon watering can. This will save you constant trips to the kitchen sink and will encourage you to give the trees the amount of water they really need.

Between waterings, never allow the soil to dry out completely unless the tree is a succulent or a cactus. Below that dry one to two inches of soil you should still be able to see dark soil and feel some dampness. Scratch down through the topsoil and take a look. If the soil is dry three or four inches down, water the container immediately.

It is also important to break up the topsoil with a fork or a spoon once or twice a month. This will help the water to seep evenly into the soil rather than pouring straight down the insides of the pot and out the drainage holes. It will also encourage the spread of oxygen to the roots. Turn the topsoil over just as you would soil in a vegetable garden.

Use tepid water when watering all your indoor trees (and smaller plants as well). This is especially important in winter when cold water from the tap can be extraordinarily cold. A sudden dose of ice-cold water applied to the soil of a tropical tree might shock the roots and severely damage the tree. Since the majority of indoor trees are tropical, it makes good sense to keep their soil fairly warm. In summer, if you are watering trees outdoors with a hose, it is not necessary to follow this rule. But do be careful in fall and winter and play it safe by always using tepid water on all your trees.

Tap water is as good as any other kind of water, and it is not necessary to boil it first or buy distilled water. However, if your system is equipped with a water-softening unit, or if the chlorine content is unusually high, you should find another source of water.

About once a year, give your trees an exceptionally thorough watering to wash out excess fertilizer from the soil. Professional growers call this process *leaching*. Fertilizers can leave harmful residues of salts which can burn the root hairs of a tree. To leach the soil, take the tree outside and soak the pot with a hose. Let the water drain out the drainage holes, then soak the pot again. Follow this procedure four or five times in a ten-minute period. If the pot does not have drainage holes, lay it on its side after every drenching and let the water run out. If you live in an apartment, leach the tree in the bathtub or the kitchen sink. If your tree is large and immovable, fertilize it only once or twice a year. This will decrease the danger of harmful salts building up.

It is also wise to leach a tree when you first bring it home. The soil may contain excess amounts of fertilizer from having had its growth sped up in Florida or Southern California.

Light

We have become acutely aware of the importance of adequate light for indoor trees this year since we moved from southern Virginia to the White Mountains of New Hampshire. Some of our trees that did beautifully in the South are struggling for survival here. It is November now, and the problem is getting worse. To complicate matters, we live in the woods. The difference between the brightness of our house in Virginia and the comparative gloominess of our house in New Hampshire is catastrophic for the plants. We will ski, skate, snowshoe, and toboggan this winter, but some of our trees and plants may not survive. They simply can't adapt to the radical change in light.

Geographical location plays a tremendous part in the intensity of light your home receives. Winter sunlight in Southern California is just as intense as summer sunlight in Maine. It is no problem growing trees indoors in Florida, but some species may have trouble in winter if you live in the Far North. It would be unthinkable to grow a weeping fig indoors in Alaska unless you kept it under strong artificial lights all day from September or October through April or May.

From personal experience, we can vouch that good lighting is essential to the growth of indoor trees. We have more sympathy now with apartment dwellers whose lighting complaints used to leave us cold. After all, we had a jungle growing in our house in Virginia. None of our trees or plants ever failed.

Life can deal worse blows than the death of indoor trees and plants, but there is something ominous and unsettling about the death of plants all the same. There is no point saying blithely, "All indoor trees are easy to grow," when in some cases they are not.

It is almost always *lack of light* that makes some species difficult to grow. Fortunately, artificial lighting can solve most low-light problems, although the cost of lighting a large tree may be prohibitive for some. The larger the tree is, the more light it needs to cover its entire foliage area. A six- or seven-foot tree will need two or three strong lights of 150 watts or more to provide all its leaves with adequate light. If the tree is in a location where it gets absolutely no natural light, it will need up to sixteen hours of artificial lighting a day.

The great thing about indoor trees, however, is that there are quite a few species which will survive in low light. The corn plant (*Dracaena fragrans massangeana*) and the *Dracaena marginata* are two of the best. We have four marginatas in New Hampshire which are doing beautifully. Other dracaenas such as the *warnecki* and the 'Janet Craig' are also excellent. The *Pleomele reflexa* (sometimes called Malaysian dracaena) is closely related to the dracaenas and is another tree to consider. Philodrendrons are renowned for their adaptability to low light. Two, the *Monstera deliciosa* and the *selloum,* are potentially huge and can be grown to look like trees. The rubber tree is practically indestructible once you learn to water it correctly. Certain palm trees, such as the kentia palm, parlor palm, and bamboo palm, actually do better in low light than in bright light. The screw pine (*Pandanus*) will live almost anywhere. And while the scheffleras do best in bright light, we have grown many with success in areas with only a moderate amount of light.

If your home is not well lit, consider these trees first. Then, if you feel you can afford to supplement natural light with a modest amount of artificial light, you can begin to grow such species as the weeping fig and the Norfolk Island pine.

We should add that it is fairly easy to grow a *small* tree that requires bright light in almost any home. A small jade tree or a citrus tree can be placed on or near a window sill and get all the light it needs. Giving indoor trees adequate light only becomes a problem when trees grow tall. One thing to consider is the height of your windows. Do not buy a tree that is taller than your windows, unless you plan to give its upper leaves artificial light.

It goes without saying that the more light your trees receive, the better and faster they will grow. Light is food. It is infinitely more important to trees than fertilizer. Light is the essential stimulus (along with carbon dioxide) which causes photosynthesis. This is the chemical process in which light and carbon dioxide trigger the manufacture of starch and sugar, which in turn feed the tree and keep it alive.

If the light level is too low, photosynthesis will not occur, leaves will yellow, fall off, and in time the tree will die.

Even trees that will tolerate low light really grow best in bright locations. A dracaena will survive almost anywhere, but it will not put on a great deal of new growth unless it is moved into a location that is at least moderately bright. Some species will get leaf burn or will wilt in direct sun (including palms, rubber trees, Norfolk Island pines, philodendrons, and dumb canes), but they still grow best in bright locations just out of range of direct sun. A gauzy curtain can be drawn between such trees and the sun, but make sure the curtain is truly thin and still lets in plenty of light. Most of these trees can tolerate direct sunlight in the winter.

Winter is the most dangerous time of year for indoor trees which require bright light. Bearing this in mind, you should move such trees as close as possible to brightly lighted windows. You may also need to provide artificial lighting for some trees for five or six hours at night, since winter days are five or six hours shorter than spring and summer days. Almost all species of indoor trees can tolerate direct sunlight in winter from Virginia on north, but palms and certain other species should be moved out of direct sunlight in late February to avoid the risk of leaf burn.

Trees that have suffered indoors during the winter from diminished light will revive in a surprisingly short time if you put them outside beginning in April or May. But be extremely careful not to leave them out overnight in case of a late frost. Never give up on an indoor tree that has lost its leaves. Put it outside and forget about it for a month. Place it in the shade at first, under a covered porch or a good shade tree, and then move it into the sun after about two weeks. Do this especially with the weeping fig and the Indian laurel. Citrus trees and Jerusalem cherry trees also react well to such treatment. Others that will benefit from spring sun are privet, *Pittosporum,* croton, yew pine, loquat, banana, and sago palm.

The ideal location for a large tree such as a weeping fig which requires fairly high light is in a room with windows facing in more than one direction. A living room with a bay window facing south and several side windows facing east would be perfect. What you must try to do for such a tree is to give it light from several sides, so that all of its leaves are getting light. Otherwise one side of the tree may lose its leaves and become bare. If the tree is getting most of its light from one window only, be sure to rotate it several times a month.

Do not be deceived by all those indoor trees in shopping malls and banks which seem to be surviving on almost no light at all. Most of them are replaced on a regular basis as they begin to die from lack of light. It's a trick.

We recently saw a fascinating example of the importance light plays in the growth of trees. It is common knowledge that trees lose their leaves in fall not just because the weather turns cold but because the days grow shorter and the sun is farther away. Then photosynthesis grinds to a halt, leaves turn red or yellow, and fall off. As we write this, in mid-November, all the leaves have fallen in New Hampshire. Even the pine trees dropped a tremendous amount of needles, blanketing roofs and back roads. Two weeks ago, around the first of November, we were returning from a party one night, driving slowly down a winding back road, when we passed beneath a blinding streetlight. Underneath the light we noticed a small oak tree that still had all its leaves. The leaves weren't brown or red, they were green. We had not been drinking enough to hallucinate their color. It suddenly struck us that because of the streetlight the oak tree had been getting extraordinary amounts of light at night and did not realize that it was fall!

A less freakish illustration of this same phenomenon is that a small tree growing in the shadow of a taller tree will sometimes turn color several weeks before the taller tree. You may see a young maple tree aflame with color in early September while all the trees surrounding it are still bright green.

Acclimatizing Trees to Indoor Light

The majority of indoor trees sold commercially are grown outdoors in southern Florida in extremely bright light. Growers may argue that their stock is raised in the shade of taller trees, but even Florida shade is unbelievably bright.

Luckily, most reputable plant stores carry indoor trees that have been partially acclimatized to shade. These trees are brought into large shade houses in Florida, where they stay for several weeks or several months depending on their size. Then they are shipped north and may spend several more weeks or months inside of greenhouses and plant stores before they are sold. The Florida shade houses are not totally effective in acclimatizing trees to shade, however, since their light is still much brighter than the light in most homes. *It is therefore entirely possible that the tree you buy may not be sufficiently hardened or acclimatized to indoor light.* Some of its leaves may yellow and drop off when you first bring it home, and in extreme cases, the tree may die.

What you can do to ensure that your newly purchased tree survives is to place it at first in the brightest window in your home. This is essential for trees which require high light. With small-leaved trees such as the weeping fig and the Indian laurel, the best solution is to keep them outside for a month or two under a covered porch or a shady tree. This means that the best time to buy such trees is in spring or summer when you can put them outside. You may not have the slightest bit of trouble with new trees if your home is bright, but problems can and do arise with new trees placed in dim locations or in light-starved homes.

If you are ever down in Florida on vacation, be especially careful about where you shop for trees. Avoid outdoor garden centers, no matter how low prices seem. Buy indoor trees at a store for indoor plants. Trees sold at garden centers are meant to be grown outdoors and have not been acclimatized to shade. Even if you see a lovely weeping fig for $15 that might cost $50 in New York, pass it up. We made this mistake when we bought a sun-grown sago palm. The tree has been an absolute disaster indoors.

Artificial Lighting

More and more indoor gardeners are turning to artificial lighting as a means of successfully growing trees and plants indoors. This is especially true of city dwellers, who often find their apartments bereft of adequate light. The use of incandescent reflector spotlights or mercury vapor lights is an extremely effective way of growing certain indoor trees that otherwise might not survive in your home. They are also helpful in supplementing natural light, especially during fall and winter when natural light may not be sufficient to maintain a high-light tree. One of the greatest benefits of artificial lighting is in interior decoration, since it allows trees to be placed where *you* want them to be, in places such as hallways without windows or corners distant from natural light, instead of the trees dictating their location to you. In short, artificial lighting frees the indoor gardener from being at the mercy of the sun.

You do not need to buy special plant-growing lights for indoor trees—any kind of bulb or fluorescent tube will do. The special "grow lights" are readily available, but they are really more useful for flowering plants than for foliage plants and trees. The most aesthetically pleasing lights are the incandescent reflector spotlights or the mercury vapor reflector spotlights. Fluorescent tubes shielded by a ceiling valance or located under a bookshelf are excellent for smaller plants, but they really have to be brought out into the open to light an entire tree, and then their appearance is rather harsh. On the other hand, fluorescent tubes burn less electricity, and last ten to twelve times longer than most incandescent bulbs.

For best results, use canister-shaped or bullet-shaped spotlight fixtures which will beam the light directly on the tree. The bulbs should have an intensity of 150 watts or more for any tree over three or four feet tall.

Mercury vapor reflector bulbs are more expensive initially than incandescent reflector bulbs, but they have a better color spectrum, last about twelve times longer, and their radiance is over twice as strong (a 150-watt mercury vapor reflector bulb produces the equivalent of almost 350 watts of incandescent lighting).

Some experts claim that incandescent lights are too hot for the leaves of plants, but this problem is easily solved by keeping the lights at a safe distance from the tree. Three to four feet away is perfectly safe. One way to determine whether the lights are too close is to feel the leaves. If they feel warm or even hot, move the light back or the tree farther away.

The tree that we have seen most frquently grown under artificial lights is the weeping fig. A six- to seven-foot weeping fig should receive artificial light from above and from the sides. One spotlight focused three or four feet above the tree will keep the upper foliage healthy, while one or more spotlights focused on the sides will provide light for the middle and lower portions of the leaves. Ideally, you could also have a spotlight on the floor focused upward for the lowest leaves. Such an arrangement can create a dramatic effect at night, since the bright lights focused on the leaves will cast intriguing shadows on the ceiling, walls, and floor. Any six-foot tree grown exclusively under artificial lights will need at least one 150-watt spotlight and preferably two.

If the tree is in a location where it receives absolutely no natural light, it will need from twelve to sixteen hours of artificial light a day. If it receives some natural light but not enough, it should get five or six hours of artificial light at night.

You can tell whether a weeping fig is healthy or light-starved by its foliage. A light-starved specimen will drop leaves and look nude. A healthy tree will of course look lush and full. In winter, if you are watering it correctly and misting its leaves regularly, and it continues to drop leaves, it probably needs more light. This is where artificial lighting is helpful. The cost is not too great if you already have a light fixture in the ceiling and only keep the spotlight on for five or six hours. You would probably have it on anyway at night to light the room.

Change bulbs or fluorescent tubes before they burn out, since their radiance decreases by as much as one half toward the end of their life.

Other Ways to Increase Light in Your Home

Wall color—The color of your walls makes a difference in the amount of light your trees receive. Dark walls—browns, navy blues, blacks, reds—absorb light, while light-colored walls—pastels and various shades of white—reflect light and increase the brightness of a room. You can create a dazzling tropical effect by painting a room bright white and filling it with indoor trees. Light-colored walls are especially important in rooms which do not get a great deal of natural light. Rooms which are naturally bright will look brilliant painted with a color called "ceiling white." Such a color may sound sterile, but once you fill the room with trees and plants, you will be amazed by the effect.

No more curtains—Another way to brighten up a room is to do away with curtains and heavy drapes. This may be impractical and indelicate in an apartment, but it does wonders for a house on private land. Indoor trees and hanging baskets can be used in the windows instead. Keep the windows clean to let in the maximum amount of light.

Brighter light bulbs—There are some people who cannot stand bright light and never use anything stronger than a 75-watt bulb. But if you are growing trees indoors, you will want to give them every extra bit of light you can. For this reason, you might consider replacing dim bulbs with three-way bulbs of 150 watts or more.

These are all suggestions that we have tried ourselves. Several of our rooms in our house in Virginia were painted with ceiling white paint. We had no curtains in the windows. In fact, we had no curtains in the entire house, just rattan shades in the bedrooms and the den. Scheffleras, *Dracaena marginata,* and ferns in hanging baskets were the only curtains between us and the outside world. Not all our rooms were painted white—one was chocolate brown, another blazing red—but the ones that were white made the house extremely bright. On sunny days, it was as if we were living by the sea.

If your house or apartment feels gloomy, try painting the walls white, adding as many indoor trees and plants as you can afford, and splashing accent colors around the rooms in the form of colorful pillows and wall hangings.

Light Requirements for Specific Plants

A rough breakdown of the lighting requirements for indoor trees follows. Please bear in mind that almost all indoor trees will grow best in a bright location. *By "high light" we mean that the tree should be placed three feet or closer to an unobstructed east or west window or five feet or closer to an unobstructed south window; "medium light" means four feet or closer to a north window, five feet or closer to an east or west window, and seven feet or closer to a south window; "low light" trees can be placed from six to ten feet back from windows at any exposure. Please note that some "high-light" trees should not get direct sun.*

HIGH LIGHT OR BETTER	MEDIUM LIGHT OR BETTER	LOW LIGHT OR BETTER
Areca palm (no direct sun)	Dumb cane	Bamboo palms
Autograph tree (no direct sun)	Fatsia	Dracaenas
Banana	Hawaiian ti	Kentia palm
Candelabra cactus	Pleomele	Parlor palm
Citrus	Pygmy date palm	Philodendron
Coffee	Rubber tree	Screw pine
Coral berry	Schefflera	
Croton		
Eucalyptus		
Fiddle-leaf fig		
Indian laurel		
Jade		
Jasmine		
Jerusalem cherry		
Loquat		
Ming tree		
Monkey-puzzle tree (no direct sun)		
Norfolk Island pine (no direct sun)		
Pencil cactus		
Pittosporum		
Poinsettia		
Ponytail		
Sago palm		
Sea grape		
Weeping fig		
Yew pine		
Yucca		

Humidity

Most indoor trees except for succulents and cactuses prefer moderately humid air to bone-dry air. In today's modern apartment buildings and some homes there are air-conditioning and humidifying systems which create a stable indoor atmosphere congenial to trees and plants. But the majority of us still live in houses and apartments where the air gets dry in winter and where static electricity makes our hair stand on end and makes us jump when we go to open doors.

Using a humidifier is perhaps the most effective way to keep air moist. If your skin feels dry all winter, and your indoor trees and plants are dropping leaves, a humidifier will help you both.

The more traditional and economical way to increase humidity for indoor trees in winter is to mist their leaves daily and group them with other trees and plants. Small attractive misters made of brass or stainless steel can be found in most plant stores and discount stores, but for tall trees you should really use a large, refillable spray container such as a Windex bottle. If you're not too busy, your trees will appreciate a daily misting. There is little point in watering the waxy leaves of a rubber tree or a schefflera but trees such as weeping fig, ming, Hawaiian ti, pleomele, tree ferns, coffee, citrus, croton, banana, privet, and others need all the humidity they can get to keep from dropping leaves. Try to mist these trees several times a week and preferably once a day to keep them in good health.

Misting not only keeps leaves green, it also discourages the presence of red spider mites. Crotons are particularly susceptible to this pest in winter unless their leaves are kept moist.

If your home is filled with indoor trees and plants, the chances are that low humidity will be no problem. All that foliage will release enough humidity to keep the air sufficiently moist.

Small trees no taller than a foot or two can be placed in a pan filled with pebbles and water. But this method of increasing humidity is totally ineffective with taller trees. If you do use pebbles and water, always be sure to keep the water level in the pan below (and not touching) the bottom of the pot. Otherwise water will seep into the drainage hole and make the soil soggy.

It may sound silly, but most trees if they are not too large will applaud a trip to the shower. The simulated rain will clean the leaves, give them the humidity they need, and chase away spider mites.

The kitchen has long been a favorite place to grow plants which require high humidity. Boiling pots and kettles fill the air with steam, water from the faucet adds more moisture to the air, and when you open the dishwasher in the middle of its cycle or just after it has gone off, you can get great clouds of steam. The kitchen is a great place to grow a banana tree. So is the bathroom. But it all depends on whether you have a large enough kitchen or bathroom to accommodate an indoor tree (a small tree, of course, can fit almost anywhere).

Above all, be sure to keep indoor trees away from heating units. Electric baseboard units and forced hot air are especially harmful to leaves. A burning fireplace will also damage foliage if a tree is standing too close by.

A newly acquired indoor tree such as a citrus or a weeping fig may suffer shock when moved from the greenhouse atmosphere of a plant store to the drier air of your home. The problem is less likely to arise in spring and summer than it is in winter, so the ideal time to buy a tree with high humidity requirements is during the warm, humid months. To ensure a smooth transition from shop to home for a tree purchased in winter, be especially solicitous to the tree the first few weeks and give its leaves a good misting at least once a day. On the other hand, do not pamper it by overwatering the soil (wait until the top one inch of soil is powder-dry), and definitely do not fertilize it!

If a newly purchased tree starts dropping leaves, even though you have been misting it, the problem may well be lack of light instead of low humidity, in which case, move it into brighter light.

Leaf drop can also be caused by overwatering, so be careful not to get your diagnosis confused. Remove the tree from its container and check to see if the root ball is overly moist.

In extreme cases, if leaf drop is severe and lack of light or overwatering is not the problem, the best solution is to wrap the tree in a clear plastic bag to create a greenhouse atmosphere. Keep the tree covered for a week or two until the problem is cured, then gradually uncover it.

It is ironic that professional growers and plant shop owners who grow trees and plants in greenhouses suffer from a dread of high humidity rather than dry air. The jungle-like humidity in a summer greenhouse can cause funguses to spread at an alarming rate and ravage a grower's entire crop.

High humidity in your own home can also trigger funguses, and this may happen in summer (but also sometimes in winter) to such trees as citruses, small-leaved ficuses, dieffenbachias, palms, and especially scheffleras. You will be able to tell if one of your trees has developed a fungus by the presence of hideous black or brown spots on some of the leaves. In some cases, the stem of the tree may also become soft and spongy. We have not had too much trouble with funguses in the past, but they do sometimes appear. If one of your trees seems to have a fungus, remove all the infected leaves immediately and cut out any damaged areas on the stem. Reduce watering until the disease clears up and, if possible, bring a fan into the room to increase ventilation. Discontinue misting the leaves if the disease crops up in winter. If the spread of fungus is really serious, use a foliar fungicide such as Zineb or Maneb on healthy leaves to prevent the fungus from destroying the tree.

In summary, indoor trees will do best in a mildly humid atmosphere, but they may suffer if the air becomes too dry or too moist. (If a tree that you have just brought home develops a fungus early on, take it back to where you bought it at once. The fungus is their responsibility, not yours.) To prevent dry leaves, leaf drop, and spider mites, mist the leaves of most indoor trees often in winter.

Temperature

A recent issue of *Cracked* magazine featured a wonderful spoof on indoor gardening called "The Cracked Guide to Plant Care." The piece contained surprisingly accurate information on plant care, but each correct statement was offset by an absurd cartoon showing people knocking their brains out trying to follow growing directions. For instance, one cartoon on temperature requirements showed a man dressed in gloves, overcoat, and a Russian fur hat standing in his freezing living room hovering over a small plant. "Look, Helen," he yells ecstatically to his shivering wife. "our Alaskan fern is thriving!" The cartoon right beside it showed a frantic housewife wearing a bikini, her face dripping with sweat, holding up a fuel bill to her husband, who was standing beside a tropical plant in his bathing suit fanning himself. "Fred," she says, "we gotta get *rid* of that tropical jungle *plant*. Last month, we spent $364 on *fuel* to keep it *warm*."

It is absurd to keep your thermostat in winter at a setting of 50 degrees or 80 degrees just to accommodate your indoor trees and plants. The majority of them are far more tolerant of high and low temperatures than you might think. We left all our trees and plants outside for a week early this fall while we were away on a trip. The temperature unexpectedly dropped into the upper 30s several nights in a row, but all the plants survived. On the other hand, if there had been a frost, many of them might have died.

The safest temperature rule to follow for most species of indoor trees is: never expose them to freezing temperatures, but do not worry if they get cool air above freezing (preferably above 40 degrees) for short periods of time. Most indoor trees will tolerate temperatures between 40 and 100 degrees without harm—just so long as there are no sudden and radical shifts in temperature. If you suddenly put a tree growing indoors at 70 degrees into 30-degree weather outside, the tree might die.

Trees will grow best with a 10-degree drop in temperature at night. A daytime temperature of 60 or 70 degrees in winter and a nighttime temperature of 50 or 60 degrees is ideal.

However, there are some indoor trees which need cooler air than most. These are: Norfolk Island pine, monkey-puzzle tree, *Pittosporum,* privet, *Podocarpus, Eucalyptus,* loquat, jasmine, silk oak, and *Fatsia japonica.* Several other plants such as the coffee tree, jade tree, and citruses really prefer cool temperatures, but they will tolerate warmer air. All of the above should ideally be placed in a cool location in winter and kept as far away from heating units as possible.

Trees such as privet and *Pittosporum* are not great lovers of the indoors anyway and prefer being outside in spring, summer, and early fall. When you bring them back inside, they may defoliate considerably at first. This is partly due to reduced light, but also to indoor temperatures, low humidity, and lack of fresh air. In fact, a plant such as privet is a prime target for a cartoon in *Cracked*. Grown as a hedge outdoors, it can survive in temperatures below zero, and it is used to getting cool air in winter when it goes dormant, so it is easy to see why it may not do too well in a warm, stuffy room.

A Norfolk Island pine will dry out almost immediately if placed too near a blazing fireplace. But it may do beautifully near an unlit fireplace because of possible cool drafts created by a faulty flu.

There are also a few trees which detest cool air and drafts. These include the banana tree, avocado tree, autograph tree, *Poinsettia,* croton, dumb cane, ming tree and fiddle-leaf fig. You don't have to set your thermostat at 80 degrees to grow them (65 degrees is fine), but be extra careful to keep them out of drafts. A drafty entranceway would be the worst place to keep any of these trees.

It may seem that we have just refuted everything we first said about temperature being no real problem for indoor trees. But if you use common sense, none of your trees should be harmed. It is bad practice to place any indoor tree right up against a heating unit. And on the other hand, sudden blasts of freezing air are not good either.

Fertilizer

Fertilizing is the least important of all the factors involved in growing a healthy indoor tree. Along with watering, it is also the most dangerous for those who overdo it. We know a woman who grew a Norfolk Island pine indoors for twenty years and never fertilized it once. On the other hand, many people kill their trees and plants by overfeeding them.

Light is the most important plant food known. Fertilizer helps, but it is vastly overrated by novices who try too hard to please their plants. We urge you to be cautious, moderate, even miserly, when feeding indoor trees.

First, never feed a newly purchased indoor tree. Wait at least six months. The soil will probably have too much fertilizer in it to begin with. To be safe, wash the soil out throughly by soaking the container with a hose (or use the bathtub or the kitchen sink).

Second, only feed mature trees once or twice a year. Do not feed them more than this unless you want them to increase in size. In that case, feed them three or four times a year, but no more.

Young indoor trees and plants can be fed every one to three months depending on the species and the type of fertilizer used. Growth is most active in spring and summer, and this is the time when fertilizer helps the most. Beginning in March or April, many species can be fed with liquid fertilizer once a month. But hold off on feeding from December through about mid-February. A fast-growing tree such as *Schefflera* can be fed once a month in spring and summer with a water-soluble fertilizer. But a slow-growing tree such as a ming should only be fed once every three or four months.

The two most prevalent kinds of plant foods on the market are the water-soluble fertilizers and the timed-release fertilizers. Water-soluble fertilizers come in either liquid or powder form and must be diluted in water (for instance, one teaspoon of fertilizer to one quart of water) before they are applied to the soil. However, they are exceptionally strong and should be diluted to half the recommended strength to be safe.

Timed-release fertilizers come in crystal or capsule form and are sprinkled into the soil and then activated each time the soil is watered. Brands such as Precise by 3-M and Magamp can be purchased in plant stores and supermarkets. We prefer them to water-soluble fertilizers, because they are effective for three or four months and feed trees more evenly. Feeding a tree with a water-soluble fertilizer is like giving it a quick shot of megavitamins. It goes straight to the roots, but it doesn't last long. Timed-release fertilizers are more like vitamins taken orally every day. They are not as strong at first and do not work as fast, but in the long run they are safer, more stable, and have a more lasting effect.

If you use a timed-release fertilizer, read the instructions on the label and do not exceed the recommended dosage. Feed young trees three or four times a year, but only feed mature trees once or twice a year.

Water-soluble fertilizers can be applied more frequently, but cut the recommended dosage in half. Feed young trees every one to two months in spring and summer, then cut back feeding to every two or three months in fall and winter. Feed mature trees once in spring and once in early fall.

Certain trees should not be fed one drop or one grain of fertilizer during the winter. This applies to woody trees such as privet, yew pine, *Pittosporum,* loquat, laurel, common fig tree, jasmine, Norfolk Island pine, and citruses. Discontinue feeding in November and do not feed again until mid-February. It is wise to reduce feeding of all your trees in fall and winter to once every two or three months so they can rest.

When repotting an indoor tree with fresh potting soil, do not fertilize it for six months after potting. Do not fertilize trees that have just been pruned. Wait a week or two for them to revive. Never fertilize a sick tree. Fertilizer will only make it sicker.

Use self-restraint when fertilizing all your indoor trees. Overfertilizing will burn root hairs or cause new growth to be rapid but weak. Trees, like people, can die from too much food.

Pruning

It takes courage to prune an indoor tree. We know, because we were terrified to prune our trees and plants for years.

As a result, all our avocado plants and rubber trees always looked spindly. Our first Jerusalem cherry tree got completely out of hand and turned into a wild bush. We knew it needed pruning, but we were too afraid to touch it. It took no courage to trim the hedges outside; we were used to suckering tomato plants. But we did not trust the trees and plants we had inside. Superstition told us to leave well enough alone. It was only after repeated trips to greenhouses and plant stores, where we saw professionals pruning plants without the slightest fear, that we finally got our nerve up and followed their example. Now we can assure you that pruning is essential for many species of indoor trees—especially when they are still young plants.

The avocado tree, the rubber tree, the fiddle-leaf fig, and the coffee tree are perfect examples of what we mean.

All four of these trees need to be pruned when young in order to develop lateral

Here's an excellent example of what should happen when you prune a very young avocado. Cutting back the seedling when it is about six inches high encourages the plant to branch, making a fuller and more attractive plant. Unfortunately plants don't always cooperate. Sometimes the plant will only send out one branch which also wants to grow straight up. Pinch that one back, too, and eventually the plant will start to branch.

This corn plant was pruned or cut back at an earlier stage to encourage branching and thus a fuller mature plant.

This rather large jade tree has not been pruned and shaped. Some people may prefer them this way, but to give this plant the appearance of a real tree the leaves need to be thinned so that the branching nature of the plant is apparent.

branches and a greater number of leaves. Otherwise they will grow straight up and have spindly stems with few or no branches and great, hideous spaces between the leaves.

An avocado plant should first be pruned when it is about six inches tall; clip it mercilessly in half. As it grows taller, the top one to two inches of the stem should be clipped off once or twice a year (if it is growing fast). When and if branches develop, the tips of these should also be pruned once or twice a year. The same rule applies for coffee plants. If you buy a coffee plant six or eight inches tall, pinch off with your fingers the top inch of growth, sacrificing the uppermost leaves and pinching just above where the second tier of leaves begins. Continue to do this once or twice a year for as long as you own the plant (and pinch the tips of the branches, too).

A large rubber tree with many branches and leaves will not need pruning for the first year. But a young rubber plant with only one stem and very few leaves should be pruned immediately if you want it to develop into a branching tree. In this case, cut off the top of the stem with a knife just above the topmost leaf (or farther down the stem if the plant is already beginning to look spindly). Prune a fiddle-leaf fig the same way.

Pruning stimulates a chemical in plants which sends out an alarm telling the plant in effect, "Damage above. Start new growth below!" Since growth at the top has been temporarily halted, the plant reacts by sending out new shoots and leaves farther down the stem or at the top. This new growth may or may not develop into branches. It often takes repeated tip prunings to force a young plant to branch. In many cases the plant rebels and says, "To heck with you. I'm growing straight up anyway!" and new growth starts again where you have pruned and the plant continues to grow straight up.

Not all indoor trees need pruning to stimulate branching and fuller growth. Flowering trees such as citruses, Jerusalem cherry trees, and some species of fig trees branch on their own. The process of flowering temporarily halts tip growth and encourages new growth below. However, if these trees are not pruned, they will eventually grow wild and may look dreadful. Prune them as you would a hedge, sculpting them with pruning shears or scissors into a tamer and more aesthetic shape.

Other trees which benefit from pruning are Indian laurel, privet, jade tree, *Eucalyptus,* jasmine, *Poinsettia, Podocarpus,* and coral berry (*Ardisia crispa*).

No special tools are required to prune an indoor tree. Scissors or a knife with a serrated edge will do as good a job as pruning shears. There is no need to sterilize the cutting tool (as some authors fastidiously suggest) or seal the wounds with powdered charcoal. Avoid breaking branches by hand, however; make a clean cut without stripping the bark.

Prune branches just above an ancillary joint (where a leaf meets the branch). To be more specific, prune the branch a quarter inch to a half inch above a leaf for best results.

Pruning can also be used, of course, to control the size of an indoor tree. If you buy a six-foot weeping fig and want to keep it at the same size, prune it once or twice a year to keep it in line. A tree-like plant such as dumb cane will grow to the ceiling unless you clip off the top of the main stem once in a while. The only reason that rubber trees sometimes get embarrassingly tall is because their owners never bother to prune them.

In short, do not be afraid to prune indoor trees. The longer a tree goes without pruning, the more shapeless and scraggly it will look. Prune leaves as well as branches to create a symmetrical form. But do not get too carried away and denude the tree. An outdoor tree or hedge will rebound from pruning much faster than an indoor tree. Control your clipping shears, but on the other hand, don't be overly cautious and get nothing accomplished at all.

The best time to prune an indoor tree is in early spring before new growth appears. The tree can then be pruned again in early fall. You may also want to clip it in midsummer if new growth is getting out of hand.

We have had wonderful results pruning scraggly plants in spring or early summer and leaving them outside to revive for a month or two. This is especially true with plants that have needed radical pruning, a real crew cut.

After pruning an indoor tree, hold off on misting, heavy watering, and fertilizing for a few weeks to allow the tree to revive.

Tree Troubles
and Their Cures

Ninety per cent of the time, indoor trees develop troubles from overwatering and lack of light. Other problems stem from low humidity, overfertilizing, underwatering, drafts, and too much heat. Diseases rarely attack healthy indoor trees. Insects are more common, but they can usually be exterminated if they are caught in time. Funguses sometimes appear on leaves and stems during the summer and can be checked with fungicides such as Captan, Zineb, or Ferbam.

All three of these problems are easier to cure if your tree is healthy to begin with. But any one of them could be the crowning blow if the tree is weak from overwatering or lack of light.

Winter is the most dangerous time of year for indoor trees. If your tree starts dropping leaves, mist the leaves more frequently and move the tree closer to strong light. You may have to supplement its light with artificial lighting at night.

In spring and summer, the most frequent problems are leaf burn from direct sunlight, insects, and funguses.

But before you jump to conclusions and decide that your tree has a deadly disease, the best thing to do is ask yourself if you are watering it correctly. Do you water it once a day, once a week, or once a month? If you water it every day, every other day, or even every third day, the problem may well be soggy soil. Remove the tree from its container and let the soil dry out for several days. Then reduce watering to once a week or less. If you water the tree once a month, it may be suffering from drought. In which case, water it more frequently.

If overwatering is not the problem, perhaps the tree is starving from lack of light. Does its growth seem stunted? Consider where the tree is standing. If the location seems suspiciously dim, move the tree into stronger light.

Stunted growth can also be caused by a pot that is too small. Remove the tree from its pot and check to see if it is root-bound. If roots fill the entire pot, transplant the tree to a container one to two inches larger and use fresh potting soil.

Trees can also suffer from shock if they are knocked over and dislodged from their pots. This happened recently to one of our palms. The accident shocked the roots and killed most of the tree. Most indoor trees are hardier than that and can take a lot of beating. But sometimes a fall can do strange things to a tree and upset its whole life rhythm.

Overfertilizing usually occurs when a new tree is fed too soon after you bring it home. Ideally, wait six months before feeding a new tree. If new growth is rapid but weak and the tree wilts, repot the tree in fresh potting soil, shaking as much of the overfertilized soil loose as possible. Also check to see if a white crust has developed on top of the soil or, if the pot is clay, if there is a white crust on the outside of the pot. Both are signs of too much fertilizer.

Another way to rid soil of excess fertilizer is to drench the pot several times in quick succession and wash the fertilizer out.

Radical shifts in temperature can cause severe and sudden leaf drop. Check to see if the tree is too close to a heating unit (electric and forced air are the worst) or too close to a drafty window or door. Watch out when you buy an indoor tree that you do not bring it home in winter in the cold trunk of your car. In 1969, we lost all our plants by leaving them overnight in a U-Haul truck. We were in the midst of moving and had stopped for the night at a motel. The temperature dropped below freezing and killed every plant we owned. This was sheer stupidity on our part, and we still kick ourselves for being so careless.

Some indoor trees can also look sickly if they are not pruned from time to time. A rubber tree, coffee tree, avocado tree, or fiddle-leaf fig may be in perfect health but still look awful from lack of pruning. The tree will look spindly and have few leaves. Tip pruning once or twice a year will stimulate new growth and improve the tree's appearance.

If your indoor tree becomes unhealthy from diseases or insects, the first thing you should do is give it a rest. Reduce the watering, do not fertilize it, and move it into lower light. These measures will temporarily slow down growth and give the tree a chance to recuperate.

Insects

Hardly any indoor gardener is ever spared the problem of insects. A year or two may pass and everything may go just fine. Then suddenly one day, half your trees and plants will be swarming with bugs. This is because once they appear, insects multiply so fast that they can spread to other trees and plants. Don't panic: if your trees are healthy, the pests can usually be controlled.

Indoor trees are bothered by insects just as outdoor trees are. No plant in creation is ever completely free of pests. In midsummer, if you look closely at a tree outside, you will notice that most of its leaves have been damaged by bugs. Certain trees, like black locust, are practically denuded of leaves by the time summer ends. But from a distance, you usually don't notice that most trees have been preyed upon by insects. They look beautifully green. Indoor trees, on the other hand, have fewer leaves, and when insects do attack them, you can often notice the difference almost immediately. So it is important to catch them before they spoil the appearance of your tree and disfigure its leaves.

Be on the alert for insects in spring and summer especially. This is when aphids, white flies, and scale go to town. Spider mites appear more frequently in winter in hot, dry rooms, although we have seen them in summer, too. The five most common types of houseplant insects are described below, where we also suggest cures. *But the real key to discouraging insects is to keep your trees clean.* Mist their leaves in winter and always keep them free of dust. In summer, if you have access to a hose, take your trees outside and hose them down. Do not use leaf polish products, mayonnaise, or oil to shine the leaves. These may clog the pores and prevent the leaves from breathing. Indoor trees grow faster if they spend the summer outdoors, but watch out! They are much more likely to be attacked by pests. One way to reduce the danger of insects indoors is to hang a No-Pest Strip near your trees. It is not a foolproof method, but it helps.

Aphids—These little green insects can be a nuisance in spring and summer, especially if you put your trees outside. They love to feast on avocado plants, but they also appear on citruses, sea grapes, dieffenbachias, and palms. They are small but visible to the naked eye, slow-moving, most often colored green, and they congregate on new green growing tips and the underside of leaves. If left too long on a tree, they will deposit a sticky substance on the leaves called honeydew, which will attract ants and eventually create a sooty black mold. Honeydew is the sticky stuff that covers your car in summer if you park it under a tree. Aphids can look so fresh and green that you may mistake them at first for new growth on your tree. But when new leaves unfold, they will come out riddled with holes and looking like Swiss cheese. The best remedy is to spray aphids off immediately with a hose or to wash them off in the sink or wipe them off with a damp cloth or a sponge. If you wipe them off, be careful not to damage the growing tips. Do not use soap and water on them; the soap may kill new growth. Be persistent. If the tree is large and the infestation serious, treat it with a chemical called Malathion. This can be found in any plant store and most discount stores.

White flies—We have had more trouble with white flies than with any other pest. They are rarely deadly, but getting rid of them takes time. They multiply at an alarming rate. Just when you think you've licked them, they come back to haunt you in great clouds. Jerusalem cherry trees, citrus trees, and coffee trees are particularly susceptible to an invasion of white flies. They are small but visible and look like gnats or tiny white moths. You will know if your tree has them, because they swarm around the leaves and fly up like a snowstorm when you shake the tree. They suck juice out of leaves, causing small yellow specks to appear where they have fed. One way to control them is to hose the tree down several times a week until they disappear. If this·method fails, resort to using Malathion. You can also enclose the tree in a plastic bag and spray it with an all-purpose insect spray. White flies usually disappear in fall as the weather gets cold.

Spider mites—These are microscopic insects that suck juice from the underside of leaves and cause foliage to turn yellowish or gray. They are insidious and can kill a tree before you even know they're there. One way of detecting spider mites is to examine unhealthy foliage for signs of webs. To be certain that the webs have not been made by ordinary spiders, shake the leaves over a piece of blank white paper. If tiny red insects appear, you have spider mites. The safest and most effective way to exterminate them is to use a systemic insecticide such as Systemic or Isotox. These insecticides cleverly go to work inside the tree and make its sap poisonous to insects. Spider mites can also be sprayed off with a hose as a preliminary measure. Be on the lookout for these insects in winter, since most kinds thrive in hot, dry air. Crotons are easy prey for spider mites, as are Norfolk Island pines, *Podocarpus,* ficus trees, and many others.

Scale—These strange insects can attack almost any indoor tree. They are easily recognized as small, round, dark, stationary, hard-shelled creatures that appear on the underside of leaves along the main veins, or at the tips of stems, and suck the sap. Like aphids, they secrete honeydew, which in turn attracts ants and causes mold. Scale can be removed by hand or with a pair of tweezers, but if the infestation is serious, the best cure is a plant spray product called Ced-O-Flora.

Mealy bugs—Mealy bugs are a soft-bodied form of scale, which appear in the axils of branches and along leaf veins. They look like little bits of white cotton. They suck sap and can cause stunted growth, defoliation, and eventual death of a tree if not controlled. If only a few appear, remove them by hand. But the best method of killing them is to treat the tree immediately with Isotox or Systemic.

Propagation

The most economical and interesting way to add new indoor trees and plants to your collection is to reproduce them from your present stock of trees and plants or from those of your friends. Indoor trees are often easier to work with than smaller plants, since many species send up new growth from their base which can be separated from the tree and planted in moist potting soil.

People who love plants are usually eager to give stem clippings away, and they also react with pride if you come right out and ask them. When a visitor remarks on the beauty of the red fruit of our Jerusalem cherry trees, we inevitably reply,

Avocados are one of the easiest plants to grow from seed. It took only a year for the plant to achieve this size and fullness.

"Listen, they're easy to grow. Why don't you try a few?" Whereupon we press two or three of the fruits in the palm of his hand, even if the person has never grown a plant in his life.

(It is easy to propagate Jerusalem cherry trees by planting one fruit or several in a pot filled with moist potting soil, sinking the fruit about a half inch below the soil, covering the pot with plastic wrap, and placing it in a bright window. Do this in spring or summer if you live in New England or other northern states but at any time of year if you live in the South. Four to six weeks later seedlings will appear, and when they reach about three inches they can be separated and transplanted into individual pots.)

Other indoor trees which can be grown easily from seed are all the citruses (especially the grapefruit) and, of course, the avocado. For more detailed information on how to grow these trees from seed, consult the individual essays.

Growing Tropical Trees from Seed

Seeds for other tropical trees are harder to come by than avocado pits or grapefruit seeds, but they can be found. There is only one seed company that we know of which advertises tropical seeds in its catalogue. If you are even vaguely interested

The silk oak (left) and false aralia (right) were both grown from seed on a screened-in porch. At a year and a half, the silk oak had reached a height of six feet and the false aralia, three and a half feet.

in trying to grow a tropical tree from seed, write the following address and ask for a catalogue:

George W. Park Seed Company, Inc.
P. O. Box 31
Greenwood, South Carolina 29647

The selection includes seeds for various species of palms, philodendrons, and schleffleras along with seeds for the rubber tree, banana, eucalyptus, silk oak, coffee, and false aralia. Do not expect immediate shipment of the seeds or perfect results when you plant them, since tropical seeds dry out fast and are only available when a fresh crop of seeds has been harvested. Growing tropical trees from seed is inexpensive and a great deal of fun. All you need is some moist potting soil, a container such as a small pot or a tin can to put the soil in, and plastic wrap to cover the top of the can once you have planted the seeds. The best time to grow such seeds is in spring or summer when the sun is bright and the air is humid and warm.

Propagation by Stem Cutting

Propagation by stem cutting is one of the easiest and most popular ways to start new plants. If the tree is large enough, you can sometimes get a sizable plant started from it in no time at all. Tall rubber trees, corn plants, *Dracaena marginata,* and dieffenbachias are adaptable to stem cutting, although air layering is probably the safest method of propagating them.

Freshly cut stems need high humidity, bright light, warm, moist soil, and warm air to put down roots. Several springs ago, we were amazed to see a fallen limb from one of our apple trees actually bloom and grow new leaves. The limb had fallen in such a way that the freshly broken end embedded itself in the moist spring ground. With the sun bright and the humidity high, the limb just kept on growing. However, do not expect your own stem cuttings to grow this easily. You may occasionally get good results by growing them any old way, but if you follow the suggestions below, your chances of success will be greatly increased:

1. Take stem cuttings during spring and summer when the tree or plant is actively growing.
2. The cutting should be at least two inches long and should be made a quarter inch to a half inch *below* a leaf joint (where a leaf or leaves join the stem). The newer and greener the cutting, the better. Use a sharp knife, scissors, or pruning shears.
3. Apply a rooting hormone powder to the cut tip of the stem to stimulate faster root growth. The powder can be purchased in tropical plant stores, garden centers, and some supermarkets and discount stores. Rooting powder is not essential, but it definitely helps.
4. Plant the cutting or cuttings in a large polyethylene bag filled halfway up with moist potting soil; an ordinary pot; or a gallon milk jug or bleach jug cut in half. Use either commercial potting soil, perlite, vermiculite or sand. Make sure the growing medium is moist.

5. Cuttings need high humidity to keep from drying out, so you must create a miniature greenhouse for them. Growing cuttings in a plastic bag is the most convenient method, since then all you have to do is knot or tie the bag shut. If you use a pot or plastic jug, you will still need to enclose it in plastic wrap or in a plastic bag. For a tall stem cutting from a rubber tree or a corn plant, use a large dry-cleaning bag and prop it up tent-like with a stick. Try to make the bag as airtight as possible to ensure maximum humidity inside.
6. Place the potted cuttings in bright light but *not* direct sunlight.
7. Keep cuttings in a warm location preferably above 70 degrees.
8. Green cuttings with soft stems will root in about ten days. Barely green cuttings with semi-hard stems will take three weeks or longer. Dark, hardwood cuttings require "seasoning" first and should spend the winter in a box filled with damp potting soil, sand, or sawdust. Take hardwood cuttings in the fall, store them for the winter in the box, then plant them in spring the same way as above.
9. You can tell if a cutting his developed roots by slipping it out of the soil after ten or twenty days and checking to see if it has roots. If it does not, replant it and wait another one to two weeks. When roots have developed, transplant the cuttings into individual pots.

Propagating trees and plants takes patience, so resist the temptation to pull the cuttings up every other day to see if they have roots. If you have used rooting hormone powder and kept them under plastic in a warm, bright location, the chances are excellent that they will grow.

Propagation from Leaf Cuttings

Trees with thick, succulent leaves such as the jade tree can be propagated by planting the stems of their leaves in moist potting soil or moist sand. The leaves themselves will not grow; they will produce babies. Each cutting will produce several new plants, not just one. Remove several healthy leaves from the tree at the point where their stems meet the branch. Plant the stem of each leaf into the soil. For best results, plant the stem at a slight angle, burying a small side portion of the leaf itself, in order to protect new growth from the sun. Place the leaf cuttings in a warm, bright location out of direct sun and cover the pot with plastic wrap. When new plants appear, separate them from the old leaf and plant each one separately.

Propagation by Division

A tree such as a schefflera sometimes develops more than one main stem and can then be propagated by division. Shake the tree loose from its container and separate the sections by hand or carefully with a knife. Then replant each in a separate pot filled with fresh potting soil and set them out of direct sunlight until the foliage revives. This method will also work with *Dracaena marginata,* which is often sold with several stems growing in one pot.

Propagation from Suckers

Trees such as the screw pine, banana, palm, and yucca develop new growth from time to time at the base of their stem. These small replicas of the parent plant are called suckers. They can be removed from the stem by cutting them off with a knife (as close as possible to the stem) and planting them in moist potting soil. Cover the pot with plastic wrap and keep the suckers in a warm, bright location out of direct sunlight. They will quickly develop roots and can then be transplanted into separate pots.

Propagation by Air Layering

Air layering is another method of propagation often used on rubber trees, scheffleras, *Dracaena marginata,* false aralias, silk oaks, and crotons when they get too tall. It is more time-consuming and takes more patience than stem cutting, but it is by far the safest method for such trees. We have yet to see a book on indoor gardening that does not illustrate air layering. On the other hand, we have only seen two or three people in our entire lives who actually tried it, perhaps because it looks so complicated and scary.

But air layering is really fairly simple. All you need is a knife, a twig or a matchstick, a package of sphagnum moss (which can be found in any plant store), a piece of plastic wrap, and rooting hormone powder (which can also be found in any plant store).

Choose a thick, healthy point on the stem and cut about halfway through it with the knife. On a tall tree, make this cut no lower than two feet down from the top. After you have made the cut, insert the twig or matchstick in it to hold the cut slightly open. Dust the cut with rooting hormone powder. Remove the sphagnum moss from its package, moisten it with tepid water, and wrap a generous amount (a good handful) around the cut. Seal the sphagnum moss in plastic wrap. Now tie the plastic wrap shut at either end with tape or string.

What you have created should look like a round, dark ball in the middle of the stem. It will not look pretty, and you may want to hide the tree. Since the best time to do air layering is in spring or summer, you should ideally move the tree outside under a covered porch or a good shade tree. New roots will grow much faster this way. But be careful for high winds that might snap the tree at the point where you have cut it.

In from one to three months, the upper part of the stem will develop its own independent root system at the point where the cut was made. You may be able to see roots growing in the moss. When you feel that an ample root system has developed, remove the plastic wrap and moss from the tree and separate the upper half of the stem from the lower half by *cutting the stem just below the roots.* Then plant the rooted stem in a pot filled with moist potting soil. Do not throw away the lower half of the stem. Keep it in its pot, cover the stem and pot with a plastic bag, and in time it will grow new leaves. Grow the new cutting in bright light but not direct sun, and keep the watering down until you are sure that it is established and strong.

Air layering is a fascinating method of propagation, but it does take longer than stem cutting. A one- to two-foot cutting from a rubber tree will wilt and not develop roots if you simply cut it off and plunge it into soil. But if you grow such a stem cutting in a plastic bag in spring or summer, it may survive. We have seen this done in Florida greenhouses, where air layering is not considered necessary. But then in Florida, growing conditions are ideal. If you want guaranteed success with tall cuttings, air layering is the safer method.

Talking to Indoor Trees—Does It Help?

After years of personal observation and many interviews, we have come to the conclusion that there is nothing wrong with talking to indoor trees. On the other hand, there is little evidence to suggest that talking to them helps. It may be therapeutic for you, in which case keep on talking. But the notion that trees understand or even care what you are saying is pure hokum.

For a change of pace, make your own tree. This lovely specimen was shaped out of wire mesh filled with sphagnum moss. A metal pole set in a wood container holds the "crown" of the tree aloft. Leaves consist of about two dozen coleus plants.

Some fascinating studies have been done, however, on plant sentience. Apparently plants can sense when they're in danger, and they also react when they are harmed. In tests conducted with a modified form of lie detector, an examiner once thought of lighting a match and moving it close to a plant to see how it reacted to the threat of fire. Before the examiner even had a chance to light the match, the plant responded by emitting hysterical vibrations on the lie detector.

If you dislike plants and feel hostile toward them, if you feel a constant urge to torment them and burn their leaves, the first thing you should do is give your plants away. In all likelihood, because you don't like plants, you tend to ignore them and treat them poorly. But whether they can actually *sense* your attitude is highly doubtful. We have plants that we don't like. We shove them off in dimly lighted corners and pretend they don't exist. And eventually they suffer—for the simple reason that we forget to water them and that we keep them in poor light.

It also frequently happens that people love their plants too much. They overwater them and overfeed them, and the plants end up by dying from too much love.

Plants and indoor trees are fairly tough and self-reliant. Getting sentimental over them may actually turn them off and in the long run do them harm.

We sometimes communicate mentally with a tree if it looks exceptionally good or exceptionally bad. We may even murmur words of reassurance when we are repotting one. But, on the whole, we find that talking with people is infinitely more stimulating.

Do Indoor Trees
Like Music?

National attention was recently drawn to experiments in which plants were grown to music. The results showed that plants reacted poorly to the blaring sound of hard rock, but they grew well to the soothing melodies of classical composers such as Mozart and Chopin.

While these experiments cannot be totally dismissed, they are a standing joke among people who earn their living by growing indoor plants and trees. If plants really grew better to Mozart, every greenhouse in America would play his string quartets day and night.

We are driven mad by the constant sound of Muzak. And yet Muzak is supposed to calm you down. Who knows, perhaps a rubber tree might love the Rolling Stones, while a delicate ming tree might come unglued listening to the same tunes. It is difficult to know what taste in music each and every species has.

However, if you live in an environment where the noise outside is unusually high, playing soothing music to your indoor trees may help. Cacophony is not good for plants (it rattles their tissues), and soothing music tends to lessen bad vibrations and block out harmful sounds.

Our guess is that tropical species would like nothing better than listening to an album composed of tropical bird calls, monkey screeches, insect sounds, and an occasional deep-throated lion or tiger roar to make them feel at home.

Pros and Cons of Putting Indoor Trees Outside

Trees grow fast indoors in spring and summer, but they grow even faster outside. The fresh air, higher humidity, and bright light does wonders for trees that have suffered during the winter indoors. Plants such as privet, pittosporum, jasmine, eucalyptus, and yew pine should really spend the whole summer outdoors. But expose them gradually to full sunlight by keeping them in shade for the first two weeks. Other trees such as palms, philodendrons, rubber trees, coffee trees, and citrus trees will burn up unless you keep them in full shade until late in the day.

The safest rules to follow when putting indoor trees outside are:

1. Do not expose any indoor tree to sunlight all at once. Check the essay on your particular tree to see if it will tolerate full sunlight. If it will, expose it gradually to full sunlight over the course of several weeks (avoid full sunlight from 11 A.M. to 4 P.M. for two full weeks).
2. Beware of spring frosts. An indoor tree may be placed outside on warm days (above 55 degrees) in March and April, *but bring the tree back inside at night without fail.* Do not leave it out at night until all danger of frost has passed.
3. Beware of autumn frosts. Do not risk keeping an indoor tree outside all night beyond September 1 in northern states such as Maine, New Hampshire, and Vermont. In more temperate states, set the deadline back to September 15 or October 1 at the latest.
4. Hose leaves daily if possible—either early in the morning or at sunset —to discourage pests. Check trees frequently for pests.
5. Follow normal watering procedures for your tree. Do not wait for the elements to do it for you.

There are some drawbacks, however, to growing indoor trees outside. Aside from the danger of sunlight burning tender leaves, the worst problem is the increase in pests. Many of our trees and plants were tormented by white flies and aphids last summer. We had to hose the plants down every day to keep them from sucking the leaves dry. A severe hailstorm riddled the leaves of two of our rubber trees. Our philodendrons wilted the second we put them in the sun.

In the end, we cursed ourselves for keeping our trees and plants outside too long. It created more problems than it solved. They would have been better off spending the majority of their time inside, with occasional trips outdoors to get their leaves washed and their soil watered with the hose.

The ideal place to grow indoor trees during the warm months is on a screened-in porch. The screening reduces the number of pests somewhat and helps shield the trees from the sun. A friend of ours has plants that have literally grown into trees in one to two summers on her screened-in porch. Her schefflera (which she started from seed) grew to over six feet in less than two years. Her false aralia and silk oak grew about four feet in the same length of time. She did have trouble with black scale on her schefflera and on a small citrus tree, but most of her trees and plants were not bothered to the same extent as ours were by bugs. If you have a screened-in porch (or a screened sun porch where you can open all the windows), try keeping some of your trees and plants out there beginning in April or May. If you leave them there through September, you will be amazed by the amount of growing they do.

Another way to grow indoor trees and plants outdoors is to plunge them into the garden in their pots. This method is most effective when using clay pots, since moisture from the ground is absorbed through the clay. Sinking pots in soil also prevents trees and plants from tipping over in winds and storms. Do not remove trees from their pots; dig a hole and sink the whole pot down into the soil. Be careful that the garden is shady for trees that get leaf burn in full sun. Also be careful not to plant trees with soft stems. A schefflera could easily snap in a cloudburst or a strong wind. But a weeping fig could take it. Water trees or plants just as you normally do inside: don't wait three weeks for the elements to do it for you. Watch out for an increase in pests, and hose the leaves down to chase them away. Do this early in the morning or at sunset to prevent leaf burn.

On a trip to New York City last summer, we were amazed to see the skating rink at Rockefeller Center converted into a beer garden and filled with a small forest of pot-grown weeping figs. A similar effect, although perhaps on a less lavish scale, can be created on your own outdoor patio with indoor trees.

What to Do When
You're Away on Trips

A clever way to keep indoor trees and plants sufficiently moist when you're away on trips is to wrap them in plastic dry-cleaning bags. The greenhouse atmosphere created by the bags will make the trees and plants grow better than they usually do. This method will keep trees and plants moist for at least two weeks. It will not work for a tree that is too large for such a bag, but it is a brilliant solution for the majority of foliage plants.

Be sure to wrap both the foliage and the pot of an indoor tree securely in the bag, and tie the bag shut like a balloon with either a knot or string. With smaller plants, place several in the same bag. Water the soil thoroughly first. Do not use brown or dark green plastic garbage bags; only a clear plastic bag will do. Otherwise the tree may die from lack of light. Place the tree in a moderate amount of light, but not in strong, direct sun. It will get too hot and possibly die from all the steam trapped inside the bag.

For trips of longer than two weeks, you will need to ask a friend or neighbor to water your trees and plants. Choosing a fairly experienced indoor gardener is important. An incompetent plant sitter will overwater everything and end up killing some of your plants. If this happens, your own hard feelings may force the friendship into a permanent decline. Pick someone whom you trust and who can follow directions. Work out a reciprocal arrangement for watering your friend's plants, too.

Do not feel overbearing or picky when giving your friend instructions about how to water each tree and plant. If anything, urge the person to go easy on the watering. Tell him especially not to water any tree until the surface of the soil dries out. And don't hesitate to be specific; write instructions down on paper if you feel it's really necessary. For instance, "The tall one by the coffee table I usually water once a week. Soak the whole pot. The little one on the desk needs water twice a week," etc.

For trips of under a week, there is no real need for either a plant sitter or plastic bags. Just water the soil of all your trees and plants well before you leave.

If you only have one or two indoor trees and few other plants, you can most likely get away with leaving them untended for ten days or even two weeks. Trees in large pots rarely need watering more than two or three times a month anyway.

In summer, if you have a covered porch or a screened-in porch, you will be astounded by the amount of new growth your trees and plants put on while you're away. Be sure the porch is well protected, however, or the plants may all blow over in a storm. And, again, even with the porch method, you will definitely need a plant sitter if you plan to be away for more than two weeks.

Bonsai

Before discussing the individual trees, we'd like to add a word about an ancient way of growing trees in containers. Long before large tropical plants became popular to grow indoors, the Japanese were growing miniature trees in shallow dishes called bonsai—which they sometimes brought indoors. We say sometimes, because the majority of bonsai are temperate climate trees. They are normally grown outdoors in a sheltered location and only brought inside for short periods of time.

Broadly speaking, any tree on earth can be trained as a bonsai. This means that all the tropical and subtropical trees we discuss are theoretically capable of having their roots and top growth pruned and being grown in small pots. But woody species are more desirable and easier to work with. Several indoor trees which can be

Bonsai is usually created with trees from a temperate climate and thus not suited to indoor display except for brief periods. But tropical plants, such as this lady palm, can make a lovely bonsai which can be enjoyed and grown indoors with little problem.

trained as bonsai are: Jerusalem cherry, citruses, privet, *Podocarpus, Pittosporum,* jade, Norfolk Island pine, monkey-puzzle tree, dwarf pomegranate, loquat, croton, coral berry, weeping fig, mistletoe fig, and ming.

Believe it or not, we accidentally created a bonsai out of one of our Jerusalem cherry trees by pruning its top growth and potting it in an oriental pot. A master bonsai artist would frown, but to our untrained eyes, the little tree looks gorgeous.

To most Americans, bonsai is still considered amazing and almost mystical, not to be learned by clumsy Western hands. But in fact most of us practice a rudimentary form of bonsai when we prune and repot our plants and trees. The miracle of bonsai is a twofold process: by trimming roots and limiting their growth in a small pot, you can stunt and limit the size of top growth; conversely, by pruning top growth you can limit the growth of the roots. We have seen a bonsai rubber tree three inches tall, complete with exposed roots and a small trunk, with leaves no larger than a quarter. By limiting the size of its container and pruning its top growth, the grower was able to produce a tree with leaves one tenth the size of ordinary rubber tree leaves.

Bonsai is a fascinating craft and worth pursuing if the notion tempts you. Many excellent books have been written on bonsai and two of the best are *Bonsai for Americans* by George F. Hull and *Bonsai—Miniature Trees* by Claude Chidamian. The *Handbook on Dwarfed Potted Trees* published by the Brooklyn Botanic Garden can be found in many plant stores and is a first-rate introduction to bonsai. The hobby is open to all, saints and sinners alike, to Americans as well as Japanese, and is not as difficult as it looks. But if you buy a ready-made bonsai, your first consideration should always be whether the tree is temperate or tropical and can be adapted to indoor living.

Part II

Trees to Grow Indoors

Autograph Tree or Fat Pork Tree

(Clusia rosea)

This is a fascinating tree with large, thick, tongue-like leaves growing on sturdy branches attached to an erect woody stem. Its structure resembles a rubber tree, but its leaves are thicker, flatter, lighter green in color, and feel more like the fleshy leaves of a succulent. The autograph tree grows to over twenty feet outdoors and takes up lots of space indoors as it matures. From the West Indies, it is a wonderful-looking tree that is becoming more and more available in sizes from one to five feet.

But watch out! Little is known about its ability to survive indoors. A large shipment of autograph trees arrived this summer at our local plant store, and within a week all their leaves turned yellow and started falling off. Perhaps the plants had just been pulled out of the ground and were not accustomed to living in either pots or shade. Or perhaps they were dramatic proof that autograph trees don't grow well indoors. A number of plant shop owners have expressed complete disappointment to us about their hardiness as indoor trees.

If you buy an autograph tree with this warning in mind, be extra careful to water it correctly and give it the right light.

Autograph tree (*Clusia rosea*).

When watering, always allow the top of the soil to become powder-dry one to two inches down depending on the size of the pot. A large container seventeen inches in diameter or more should not be watered until the soil is dry two inches down. One inch down is a good rule of thumb for trees in pots twelve to sixteen inches. With smaller pots, you should be able to pick up enough dry surface soil to sift through your hand. Water the tree thoroughly, allowing all the soil in the pot to become moist, then empty the drainage dish in which the pot stands.

Keep the autograph tree in curtain-filtered light or in bright indirect light against a light wall. Do not expose it to direct sunlight in summer, especially hot sun coming from the south. Winter sun won't do it any harm.

The tree can grow a foot or more a year indoors—if you can keep it alive. Fertilize it with a timed-release fertilizer following directions on the label. Or use a water-soluble plant food once a month through spring and summer, then discontinue feeding in the winter. Only fertilize the tree once or twice a year if you wish to contain its size.

Keep the autograph tree in a warm room where the temperature rarely falls below 55 degrees.

The tree gets the first of its colorful common names from the fact that one can write on its leaves with a pen. The writing will remain engraved on the leaves without doing them any harm. The second of its common names, fat pork tree, is more mysterious and may or may not have something to do with the fleshy texture of the leaves.

Propagate the autograph tree in spring or summer by air layering (see page 50) or by clipping the top eight inches off the main stem and planting it in moist potting soil covered by a plastic bag.

Avocado Tree
(Persea americana) also known as alligator pear

About five years ago, we got a tip from a friend on how to grow an avocado tree indoors. "You have to start the pit in a dark place," she said. "The pit hates light. Put it in a cupboard or a closet." Like fools, we took her advice and wasted two years of our time. We riddled a pit with toothpicks, sank it in a glass of water, and put it in the basement on a shelf. Then, just to be safe, we locked another pit up in a kitchen cabinet and put a third one on a shelf in the front hall closet. We were so paranoid about exposing the pits to light that we rarely used the basement, the kitchen cabinet, or the front hall closet. It was as if we were trying to develop film.

A year passed and nothing happened. At the end of the second year, having thrown two of the pits away and lost track of the third, we were cleaning out the basement one day when we stumbled on the old pit on the shelf. To our astonishment, it had grown a stem about three feet tall, at the end of which was one live leaf!

It was then that we decided to go out, buy a book, and find out how the indoor avocado tree is really grown.

Avocado tree (*Persea americana*).

We know of no better book on the secrets of indoor avocado growing than Hazel Perper's witty and accurate *The Avocado Pit Grower's Indoor How-to Book*. We started following her advice three years ago and now have seven avocado trees flourishing in our house. They are not the most attractive plants on earth (who doesn't remember his mother or his friend's mother growing some strange, leathery kind of plant in a glass on the kitchen window sill), but in spite of that they are interesting and strangely satisfying to grow. Few people would ever dream of buying an avocado tree in a plant store, but a gleam of pride comes into their eyes when they look at their own avocado pit growing on the shelf.

There are a number of different ways to grow the pit. One popular method is to plunge it base down into moist potting soil. We will explain this method shortly, but first let us tell you how we grow ours.

Once we have eaten the fruit, the first thing we do is rinse the pit off in tepid water and peel off what remains of its brown skin. It is essential to use tepid water on the avocado at all times since it is from the tropics (Mexico, Guatemala, and the West Indies originally) and can't stand cold. If you leave the skin on the pit, the roots will have a harder time emerging and the pit may never grow.

Now we fill a glass or cup with tepid water. Then we insert three or four toothpicks around the middle of the pit and lower it base down into the water. The base of the pit is usually the wider, flatter end. If your pit is a perfect sphere, look for signs of a dimple at one end. Now, having set the pit in the water, with the tooth-picks balancing on the rim of the glass and the upper half of the pit exposed to the air, we simply place the glass on a window sill and wait.

Hazel Perper claims that the pits develop a better root system in low light, but our pits usually get some sunlight every day and do fine. On the other hand, we have also grown them on the counter in the shade, and they grew just as well down there.

At this point the pit can take anywhere from a few days to a month to produce its first roots. Be patient. Check the water level in the glass every day and replenish it with tepid water up to the middle of the pit. Once the roots appear, the pit will gradually start to split apart. Through this split will grow the stem. This whole process takes time. The glass may actually fill up solid with an intricate system of white roots before the stem appears. We are used to waiting about six weeks for the stem to appear from the time we first submerge the pit in water.

Now comes the hard part, for you must perform a seemingly murderous act. Having waited all this time for the stem to appear, let it grow about six inches tall and then *clip* it in half. Cut it with a pair of scissors. This must be done in order to produce a tough, thick, freely branching stem. Otherwise you will have what we had in our basement, a long skinny stem topped by one pathetic leaf.

Don't worry. Clipping the stem in half won't kill the plant, no matter what you think. Within two weeks it will send up a new branch just below the cut, or it will fork into two branches if you're very lucky.

Now you can pot the plant.

Use six-inch or eight-inch pots at first and store-bought potting soil. Fill the bottom of the pot with soil, remove the toothpicks from the pit, lower the pit and roots carefully into the soil, and add more soil around the sides of the pit, but keep the upper half of the pit above the ground. Give the soil a good watering and place the plant in a window with bright, but not scorching, light. Water the young plant with tepid water once a day. As the plant matures, you can cut the watering back to twice a week. You need not fertilize the soil for the first six months, since the plant gets all its nourishment when young from the decomposing pit.

Some avocado trees grow incredibly fast once they've started. The tree pictured in the photograph is over five feet tall and less than a year and a half old. But it was grown on a screened-in porch and got the benefit of the outdoors for two full springs and summers. Indoors the tree grows slower, but the roots keep growing fast. You may have to transplant the pit to a ten-inch pot within a month or two of its first potting. Do this if growth suddenly slows down. In all likelihood, this means the roots are pot-bound.

When the young plant is about a foot high, clip one or two inches off the top. Also prune lower leaves or branches to keep the plant looking symmetrical. The more pruning you do, the more growth you will stimulate from below. Pruning is the key to keeping the avocado tree from looking spindly. It takes courage, but it must be done.

An unusually hardy avocado plant will grow to the ceiling if you let it. There used to be an enormous avocado tree growing in the Andover Academy library that rose almost two stories!

We tried putting our young avocado plants outdoors last summer, but the leaves turned bronze in the sun and aphids attacked the growing tips, while white flies feasted on the leaves. A screened-in porch would have been much better. Be careful. If you want to put the plant outdoors, keep it in the shade and water its leaves often to prevent pests. You can kill aphids, scale, and thrips with Malathion spray, but weaken the recommended dosage, especially on younger plants.

Growing avocado pits directly in soil is simpler than the water method, but then you can't see the roots growing in the glass, and you never know what's going on down there below the soil. In this sense, the soil method is more tantalizing and takes more patience. First, peel the brown skin off the pit and rinse it under tepid water. Fill a small pot or tin can with moist potting soil (sand, vermiculite or perlite will also work). Do not use garden loam—it dries out much too fast. Plant the pit base down in the soil, leaving its upper half exposed to the air. Place the pot in a warm, sunny window and water the soil daily. The pit should split apart and sprout in six to eight weeks. Be patient. When the sprout reaches six inches, clip it in half. New growth will appear in about two weeks. From now on, keep the plant in a bright location, but out of range of scorching sun.

Growing avocado trees indoors is not only fascinating but inexpensive. Experiment with them and play the odds. The more pits you have growing at once, the more failures you can afford to have. You can collect the pits and keep them in the kitchen for a month or longer before you actually put them into water or soil. Some pits will not grow, no matter what you do, so don't always blame yourself.

In the winter, keep your avocado tree away from cold windows and out of drafts. The tree will die in temperatures much below 40 degrees.

You have probably noticed that some avocados are dark and rough-skinned while others are shiny and bright green. The rough-skinned avocado, or alligator pear, is grown in Florida. Connoisseurs prefer its taste to the shiny California avocado, which they scornfully call "plastic fruit." We have found the Florida avocado easier to grow indoors, since it often has a larger pit which cracks more easily.

Alas, we have never heard of anybody's indoor avocado tree actually bearing fruit.

Banana Tree

(*Musa nana* or *M. cavendishii*) commonly called Chinese dwarf banana

Few indoor trees can match the dwarf banana for sheer impact. From southern China, this is a large, impressive plant in spite of its diminutive common name. Mature specimens grow four to five feet tall with broad leaves, three feet long. The only trouble with the dwarf banana is that it can look rather ugly unless it receives ideal care. Its leaves have a tendency to turn brown and ragged at the edges (even outdoors). Young plants are usually greener and better-looking than tall speci-

Dwarf banana tree (*Musa nana*).

mens. Still, if you like to grow uncommon plants, the banana tree is worth tracking down. While it is not a standard item in most plant stores, it can be found. It will grow indoors if you provide it with the right conditions, and if you have the space.

The plant gets its generic name, *Musa nana,* from Antonio Musa, who was court physician to Augustus Caesar. *Nana* is Latin for "dwarf." The dwarf banana is a member of a distinguished family (Musaceae) which contains the largest herbs in the world. For instance, the common yellow banana (*Musa sapientum*) has leaves ten feet long and grows thirty feet tall. It boggles the mind to realize that once this enormous herb bears fruit, it then behaves as most herbs do, and dies. New growth then begins again from the underground stem. The largest member of the family is the ravenala, or traveler's tree of Madagascar, which actually remains a tree and has an amazing upright leaf spread resembling a lady's fan.

The dwarf banana really requires a greenhouse to look its best. It will grow indoors under normal house conditions, but for how long is anybody's guess. Some friends of ours have one growing in their bathroom, and it looks spectacular there (they have five children and the bathtub is in constant use, so the air is always thick with steam). The tree needs high humidity, very bright light, and a great deal of warmth. It may die in temperatures below 60 degrees. The more humid the air, the better. The tree has a voracious appetite during its growing season and can be fertilized as often as once or twice a week at that time. Use ordinary potting soil or peat moss when repotting.

The best time to buy a dwarf banana is in late spring or early summer when growing conditions indoors are ideal. That way the plant will look its best for at least five or six months. If it deteriorates in the fall when you turn on the heat, you can chop the plant down, pull it from its pot, shake the soil loose from the bulb and roots, let it dry out for about one week, and then wrap the bulb in dry peat moss and store it in a dim place where the temperature does not drop below freezing. Do not wrap the bulb and the peat moss in a plastic bag or the plant will suffocate. Leave the dry bulb dormant until spring. When the weather warms up, plant the bulb in moist (but not soaking wet) potting soil, and put the pot outside. Go easy on the watering until new growth appears above the soil. Then commence to water the plant regularly, keeping the soil constantly moist but not soggy. As the temperatures rise into the 80s and 90s, the plant will rapidly grow back into a handsome tree. Watch out for high winds and pouring rain, since its soft leaves tear easily. The original root will last almost indefinitely and can be planted, chopped down, and stored in the above manner year after year.

Although this procedure may sound too involved and complicated it really works. It is not much different than planting tulip bulbs. Many outdoor gardeners plant dwarf bananas in their gardens, where the trees thrive and add a wonderful exotic touch all summer long. We have seen banana plants growing outdoors in the summer as far north as New Hampshire.

Other species of banana sometimes grown indoors, but which also need high humidity and bright light to do well, are *Musa x paradisiaca,* with leaves up to six feet long, and *Musa zebrina,* or blood banana.

Candelabra Cactus
(Euphorbia lactea)

The candelabra cactus is a striking succulent which looks especially attractive when set off by itself against a bare white wall. Named for the candelabra-like spread of its green-and-white-striped branches, the plant grows twenty feet high or more in its native India and is sometimes planted as a hedge in southern Florida and the tropics. It is widely available as a one-to-two-foot pot plant, but harder to find as a mature tree. Like most euphorbias, it is slow-growing but extremely hardy indoors.

Give the tree direct sunlight, preferably at a south window, or bright indirect light against a light wall. If natural light is unavailable, use a 150-watt bulb focused three feet above the tree for at least twelve hours a day.

The candelabra cactus will rot if it is overwatered, so be especially careful to let the soil become dry between thorough waterings. Let the top one to two inches of soil become powder-dry. Always use tepid water, and never let the pot stand in water. In fall and winter, the tree will undergo a dormant period and should only be watered enough to keep it from shriveling. Night temperatures of 55 to 65 are ideal in winter, but the tree should be able to survive under warmer conditions.

Do not fertilize a newly purchased candelabra cactus for the first year. Then only feed it once a year in early spring.

Candelabra cactus (*Euphorbia lactea*). (Photo by
Terrestris, N.Y.C.)

When repotting, use commercial potting soil or a blend of half sharp sand and
potting soil. A porous clay pot with a central drainage hole is the safest container
to use. After repotting, do not water the tree for a week or two until its roots become established.

Like other succulents, the candelabra cactus is easy to propagate by cuttings.
The best time to do this is in the spring. Make the cutting anywhere along a
branch, using a sharp knife. Wash the milky sap off the bottom of the cutting and
let the cutting callus for a week or two in a cool, shady place. Then plant the cutting in barely moist sand or in a mixture of potting soil and sand. Do not sink the
cutting deep into the soil—just enough to hold it upright (otherwise it may rot).
Grow the cutting in a warm, semi-shaded spot and keep the soil barely moist until
the plant shows signs of new life.

The candelabra *cactus* is easily confused with the candelabra *tree, Euphorbia
ingens,* which hails from South Africa. The latter is not as widely available in
stores and is generally thicker, and lacks the white stripe down the center of its
branches. Both species produce a milky sap which can be mildly poisonous, and
both require the same care indoors.

One of the most fascinating euphorbias we have come across is *E. lactea cris-
tata,* commonly known as elkhorn or frilled fan, but which we prefer to call "brain
cactus." As a mature tree, it has a thick, woody trunk and a huge, grotesque crown
of intricate succulent growth which bears an almost horrifying resemblance to

brain matter. We saw several large specimens about five feet tall at a cactus nursery in Florida last year, but we have not run across any large ones at plant stores in the north. The brain cactus is worth searching for if you are looking for a highly unusual tree. It, too, requires the same care as the candelabra cactus.

All three of the euphorbias mentioned here are extremely slow-growing and should be bought large if you want to display them as trees. Prices vary from store to store, but be prepared to spend $20 or more for specimens over three feet.

Citrus Trees

(Citrus mitis, C. paradisi, C. ponderosa, C. taitensis, Fortunella margarita)

Few houseplants are more tempting to buy than a small green citrus tree loaded down with bright shiny oranges. The tree makes a beautiful gift at Christmas or any other time. But appearances can be deceiving. While the tree is an ideal florist's plant, it is tricky to keep alive for more than six months or a year unless you get to know its habits and give it proper care.

We do not recommend your buying a tall, expensive citrus tree (five feet high or more) unless you can provide it with a greenhouse, or unless you live in a warm climate where the tree can be grown on an outdoor patio nearly year-round. Citruses must have strong direct sunlight and even watering—and preferably cool night temperatures in fall and winter—to thrive. Anything short of optimum conditions can easily result in defoliation and the eventual loss of the tree.

We know a family who have a magnificent eight-foot grapefruit tree which they grew from seed. The tree stands in their living room and is about twenty-five years old. On the other hand, we are more accustomed to seeing people's citrus trees with a few little oranges clinging bravely to branches practically devoid of leaves.

The problem is usually lack of light and incorrect watering.

All citrus trees should receive the best sunlight available when indoors. Too much shade inside and the leaves will drop. The best location is in a window which faces south. Place the tree near the window, either on the sill or on a table up against the sill. A room painted white will increase the amount of light the tree receives. An east window which gets full morning sun is also good. If natural light is unavailable, use a 150-watt bulb focused three feet above the plant for at least twelve hours a day.

When watering, always keep the soil moist. A dry citrus tree will not forgive you. Don't drown the plant, but find a happy medium. If the soil is too soggy, the leaves will curl and drop off. If it's too dry, they will also wither and drop off. As a friend from Chicago writes: "You have to get to *know* your citrus plant. (I don't know anything about talking to them! I just curse them when one of the thorny spines pierces my skin.)" The plants require more water in spring and summer than they do in fall and winter, when they undergo a dormant period. Mist the leaves in winter as often as you can.

Citrus tree (*Citrus mitis*). (Photo by Terrestris, N.Y.C.)

In the summer, take your citrus plants outside. This is the best formula for keeping them healthy and making them grow well. Avoid exposing them to direct sunlight, and keep them in the shade of a porch or under a tree. Bring them in before the first frost without fail!

In the winter, they do best with night temperatures around 60 degrees.

The next time you cut a grapefruit, orange, lemon, or lime open, you should really try growing some of the seeds. The best time to do this is in spring or summer; in winter the seeds just take too long to sprout. All you need is a pot or a tin can, moist potting soil—and patience. Any seeds will do, although the easiest to grow are ones that have already germinated inside the fruit. The older and soggier the fruit, the better. The only reason people fail at growing citrus seeds indoors is that they give up on them too soon. It takes anywhere from two weeks to a month or longer for seeds to sprout, so just sit back and take your time.

Use a small container filled with commercial potting soil. Avoid garden loam, as it dries out and hardens much too fast. Then cover the pot with plastic wrap. Place the pot in a bright window, and check the soil once a week to make sure that it's still moist.

Do not expect all the seeds to sprout. The more seeds you plant, the better your chances of success. Once the seeds have sprouted, move the pot out of scorching light, but still keep it in a bright place. Water the soil often. Growth will be rapid and satisfying at first (the seedlings will grow perhaps two inches in the first few weeks), then it will slow to a snail's pace for the first year. Do not expect a seedling to grow more than about a foot for two years. If you are patient enough to wait five years, you will have the satisfaction of having a small tree. Keep the plant pruned to encourage branching, and repot with commercial potting soil when roots become pot-bound.

Citrus trees prefer an acid soil, although adding acid to the soil is not always safe and not imperative. If you have several citruses growing at once, try this experiment on one of them: dilute a tablespoon of cider vinegar in a quart of water; water the plant twice a year, but no more, with this solution. It should do wonders for the plant if you have not made the solution too strong or overwatered the plant. Another way of adding acid is to use German peat moss when repotting. German peat has a higher acid content than ordinary potting soil.

Our friend from Chicago, who has been growing citrus trees indoors for twenty-five years, has this to say about his own experiences with growing a grapefruit tree from seed:

> The tree has suffered through some rather harrowing problems. The worst was incurred the time I put it on a dolly, hauled it into the garage, left it there for a while, and during a cold snap, with the garage door open, it was frostbitten; lost all of its leaves, and appeared very much to be a goner. So I cut it down severely, leaving about eight inches of the trunk, and took it up to my living room, southeast corner, fed it some liquid plant food, and by golly, it started to leaf feebly. In the warm spring, I took it outside, and it did beautifully, and is now about six feet high. I found out that it is tough on the plant, when it is taken outside in the spring, to put it in the direct sunlight, because it gets a sunburn. The leaves turn yellow, drop off, and otherwise give a messy appearance. During the past few years, I have put it beneath a spreading ash tree where it gets plenty of late afternoon direct sun, and it has done quite well.

He also reports that he has "two plants grown from lime seeds; another pot has a larger tree grown from grapefruit; and about three months ago, I started some plants from seeds of a miniature orange tree such as you purchase in garden shops or through the mail. I got the seeds from a tree my young nephew bought."

The hardiest species of citrus tree available in plant stores is the calamondin or Panama orange, *Citrus mitis,* which grows to about two feet. The ponderosa lemon, or *C. ponderosa,* will eventually reach eight feet and produces a few very large lemons resembling grapefruit. Other varieties available are the Otaheite orange, *C. taitensis,* and the kumquat, *Fortunella margarita.* The grapefruit, *C. paradisi,* is not usually available in stores and is best grown from seed.

Citrus trees are susceptible to a number of pests, including white flies, spider mites, mealy bugs, aphids, and scale. Keep the leaves well washed during the summer to discourage them from feeding on the leaves. Malathion will help control aphids, scale, and mealy bugs, while white flies and spider mites will partially succumb to Isotox or Systemic.

The trees may grow six inches to a foot in a year with fresh air in the summer, good strong light indoors, and the correct amount of water. Feed with a timed-release fertilizer following instructions on the label, or use a water-soluble plant food diluted to half the recommended strength every two months.

Coffee Tree
(Coffea arabica)

Two small lovely Arabian coffee plants are sitting in the window near our desk. Their upper leaves are shiny and light green, elliptical, pointed at the tips, and look remarkably like the leaves of a citrus tree. This is no coincidence, since the coffee tree is a member of the citrus family. The lower leaves are different. They are more or less round.

The plants arrived mysteriously in the mail four months ago from central Florida. They were shipped to us by a well-known coffee manufacturer. We had often seen their ads for the plants in magazines. You can send the company two labels from their jars along with a nominal fee and receive a coffee tree. Some friends who drink the brand must have peeled two labels off and ordered us the plants. We had been meaning to do this ourselves, but feared we might get sickly plants. But the plants arrived in perfect shape, so we have no qualms about recommending this procedure to you. Whoever sent us the plants, thanks!

There are several species of coffee trees, but the Arabian is the one most com-

Coffee tree (*Coffea arabica*). (Photo by George Taloumis)

monly grown indoors. It originally grew in Ethiopia and Angola but is grown commercially now in tropical America as well. Outside it grows to fifteen feet. Indoors
it will grow a foot or more a year. But it needs judicious pruning to be kept from
looking scraggly.

The plant will sometimes blossom indoors with white, fragrant flowers when it
reaches about three feet. Mist the blossoms daily to prevent them from blasting.
Green berries will then appear which will turn red as they mature. Inside the berries you will find two coffee beans. From then on, you can begin to grow new trees
yourself. Or you can hoard the beans, toast them in the oven, grind them up, and
make yourself a cup of coffee. At least one of the reasons that coffee costs so much
is that it takes a year's crop from a mature tree to yield just one pound of coffee.

The coffee tree can be tricky to grow indoors. It looks beautiful as a small plant,
but we have not seen very many handsome mature trees. They tend to be leggy
and skimpy-leaved, and the foliage bruises easily and often becomes dry and
yellowish or brown. They need high light but will burn in direct, scorching sun.
The soil should be kept evenly moist but not soggy. Allow the surface of the soil to
dry out between waterings. Commercial potting soil is the best growing medium. In
the winter you should mist the leaves every day to keep them healthy and clean.
Feed them every one to two months with a weak solution of water-soluble fertilizer. But do not feed them through December and January, and reduce the watering then so they can rest.

To avoid growing a leggy tree, you should regularly prune or "pinch off" the
plant. This can be done twice a year in early spring and early fall by snipping off
the top one to two inches of the plant. If you are miserly and only pinch off a tiny
bit, your chances of success will be reduced. Pruning is the only way to make the
coffee tree look even moderately handsome once it has outgrown its beautiful baby
stage.

If you buy a seedling rather than a full-grown tree, the best place to put it is on a
screened-in porch or outside in the shade. It will grow at least twice as fast outdoors. But bring it back inside as soon as the temperature drops below about 50
degrees. Transplant the seedling to an eight-inch pot after you have owned it for
about five months.

Coral Berry

(Ardisia crispa)

The coral berry is widely available as a small pot plant with shiny, dark green
leaves. It looks its best in spring and summer when it produces clusters of small
pink-white flowers followed by bright red holly-like berries. The plant is beautiful
when young and will eventually grow into a three- or four-foot tree. Unfortunately,
it may look rather leggy if it reaches this size without careful pruning. The best
way to grow it is to snip off the top inch of its stems about twice a year. If you
don't, it will look almost exactly like a badly grown avocado tree as it matures.

Coral berry (*Ardisia crispa*).

If you look for a tree-size coral berry in ten plant stores, you might be able to find it in one or two. Most stores are aware of its deficiencies as a large plant, and they simply will not handle it. In short, you will have to grow a tree-size coral berry on your own. We have seen several specimens which looked beautiful as small trees, but only because their owners kept them pruned.

The coral berry needs evenly moist but not soggy soil to grow well. Allow the surface of the soil to dry out between waterings. Mist its leaves in fall and winter, but discontinue misting in early spring to encourage its pollen to spread. You can help pollination along by shaking the plant or by putting it outside in the shade and letting the bees do the work. It will grow faster outside or on a screened-in porch and should be fertilized during its growing period with either a timed-release plant food (applied according to instructions on the label) or a water-soluble plant food administered once a month. No feeding is necessary during fall and winter.

Keep the plant in bright curtain-filtered light or indirect light against a light wall. Its leaves will burn and start falling off in direct spring or summer sun, but it can tolerate sunlight in the winter.

If your coral berry gets too leggy, you can air-layer it (see page 50) and start a smaller and more aesthetic-looking tree.

The coral berry likes average to cool temperatures and should be kept away from heating units in winter to prevent its leaves from drying out. It will tolerate temperatures down to 40 degrees, but night temperatures from 60 to 70 degrees in winter will suit it fine.

Croton
(Codiaeum variegatum)

We include the croton for only one reason—to warn you against buying a large one, unless you have a greenhouse in your home. Crotons need extremely bright light, warm air, good air circulation, and high humidity to look their best. They will survive in dimmer light and drier air, but they will lose their color and may look very poor. Most plant stores sell small crotons and avoid the larger specimens, mainly because large crotons tend to have long skinny stems and too few leaves. To keep your own small crotons looking fit, you should prune them once or twice a year, snipping off the top one to two inches of each stem. Otherwise you will eventually have leggy plants.

There are well over one hundred varieties of croton, most of them native to India and Indonesia, ranging in colors from dark green through bright pure yellow to orange and red. They make spectacular bushes and small trees in the greenhouse or outside. But when deprived of proper conditions, their leaves often turn a dark unhealthy red verging on black, and their texture becomes crackly and dry.

Croton (*Codiaeum variegatum*). (Photo by T. H. Everett)

State horticulturists in Florida have recently been experimenting with raising crotons in 80 per cent shade. The result so far has been a healthy plant with handsome green leaves, but little color. Still, at least they will hold up indoors.

Always keep your crotons in the brightest light in your home. Direct sunlight coming from the south is the best exposure to grow them in. Provide the most humidity you can for crotons in the winter. Small plants will benefit from having their pots kept in a tray filled with pebbles and water. Mist the foliage every day. Crotons are extremely susceptible to spider mites, and dry foliage invites trouble. Group crotons near other plants to create a more humid atmosphere. Or, if you have one, keep your humidifier going in the same room.

Crotons need moist soil in spring, summer, and early fall, but reduce the watering severely in late fall and winter so they can rest. During the warm months, keep the soil evenly moist but not wet. Do not water the soil until the surface becomes dry. In winter, wait about two weeks longer than you normally would to water.

The plants can be fertilized every two months with a water-soluble fertilizer for rapid growth or only twice a year to contain their size. A timed-release fertilizer will provide the most even feeding (follow the instructions on the label).

Use Isotox or Systemic to control severe infestations of spider mites. Otherwise, wash the leaves with a mild solution of Ivory soap and tepid water several times a week.

Keep the plants in a room where the temperature does not drop below 60 degrees. The ideal temperature for crotons is 70 degrees and up.

Dracaenas

You can't go wrong if you choose a dracaena for your first attempt at growing indoor trees. Dracaenas are great confidence builders. They require a minimum amount of care, and with correct watering, they will live for years. Bugs won't hurt them and hot air won't dry them out. Even if you live in a basement apartment or if all your windows face onto an air shaft, there will still be enough light available to maintain one of these trees. It almost seems as if dracaenas were created to be grown indoors.

Dracaena means "female dragon" in Greek, but don't let the meaning of the name put you off. The trees are extremely rugged but not hostile. There are about eighty different kinds of trees and plants in the genus *Dracaena,* the majority of them native to Africa and belonging to the Liliaceae or lily family. The lily family includes such hardy plants as the yucca tree, the ponytail palm, the pleomeles, and the Hawaiian ti plant. It is a bonanza for the indoor gardener since it offers such a wide variety of long-lived trees and plants.

The two most popular dracaenas to grow as indoor trees are the corn plant (*D. fragrans massangeana*) and *Dracaena marginata.* Separate essays are devoted to the care of these two trees. Other species which are also widely available and just as easy to grow indoors are:

Dragon tree (*D. draco*)—From the Canary Islands, the dragon tree can grow to mammoth proportions with a trunk twenty feet thick and sixty feet tall. Indoor specimens are sometimes available up to five or six feet. The leaves of the dragon tree are thick and fleshy, sword-shaped, pointed, and colored blue-gray or silver-gray. The margins of the leaves turn red in sunlight. The dark red resinous sap of this tree was believed to be dragon's blood in ancient times.

Hookeriana (*D. hookeriana*)—A handsome tree from Natal and the Cape of Good Hope, it has a slender, erect, cane-like stalk topped by a rosette of thick, shiny, sword-shaped leaves. It looks somewhat like the corn plant but has thicker, more succulent leaves. It rarely grows above six feet.

Leather dracaena (*Dracaena hookeriana*).

'*Janet Craig*' *dracaena* (*D. deremensis* 'Janet Craig')—A hybrid variety developed from the *Dracaena warneckei,* this is one of the most attractive tree-like dracaenas. It differs from the corn plant in that its large, dark green, corrugated leaves grow all the way up and down the stalk, but the leaves have much the same long, broad shape as the leaves of the corn plant. The 'Janet Craig' is extremely durable indoors and gives a fresh appearance.

Warneckei (*D. deremensis warneckei*)—This dracaena can instantly be recognized by the pure white and dark green stripes on its long, slender, pointed leaves. Tall specimens up to four or five feet are available, but they do not look exactly like trees. The leaves grow all the way up and down the stalk, and it has no trunk to speak of. Like the 'Janet Craig,' it presents a lush, striking appearance and is very hardy indoors.

Striped dracaena (*Dracaena deremensis warneckei*).
(Photo by McDonald/Mulligan)

All of these trees will grow best if you give them the following care:

1. *Watering*—Always allow the top of the soil to dry out between thorough waterings. Never water a dracaena if the top of the soil looks dark and still feels moist. When in doubt, don't water. While many indoor trees need water as soon as the top of the soil turns ashy and gray, dracaenas can actually wait a little longer. Specifically, if the pot is seventeen inches or larger in diameter, don't add water until the soil is dry two inches down. In a pot twelve to sixteen inches, water when dry one inch down. In smaller pots, wait until you can scratch up enough dry surface soil to sift through your hand. By "thorough waterings," we mean soak the whole pot; make sure all the soil gets moist. Then let excess water drain off, and always empty the dish in which the pot stands. Use tepid water when watering.

2. *Lighting*—Dracaenas will live in low light, which makes them ideal for locations where other houseplants won't survive. They are perfect for a dimly lit apartment or front hall. The trees are versatile, however, and can also stand bright light and even direct sunlight (except from the south) most of the year. For rapid growth, keep them in a bright window. For slower growth, move them into shade.

3. *Fertilizing*—A timed-release fertilizer used according to the instructions on the label will promote the most even and active growth. Water-soluble fertilizers

can be applied every two months year-round. For slower growth, only fertilize once or twice a year.

4. *Temperature*—Dracaenas prefer a warm location, but they can tolerate cold down to about 40 degrees for a short period of time. Never expose them to frost. They do *not* need cool night temperatures in winter, unlike some trees.

5. *Repotting*—Use ordinary commercial potting soil and step up the size of the container by two or three inches every three or four years. Dracaenas do best in fairly small pots. If the tree is in low light and you do not want it to increase in size, repot it in the same container but change its soil every five or six years.

6. *Fresh air*—The fastest way to make a dracaena grow is to put it outside in spring or summer. Always keep it in a shady location such as under a tree or a covered porch. Do not expect overwhelmingly rapid growth with any of these trees; six to ten inches a year is average to good, and twelve inches or more a year is superior. The trees can be plunged into the soil in their pots if you can find a shady garden spot.

7. *Aerating*—Break up the top of the soil with a fork on a regular basis to help the soil breathe air and absorb water.

8. *Propagating*—The easiest way to propagate a dracaena is to cut off the top of the stem below the foliage and plant the cutting in moist, but not soggy, potting soil (sand, vermiculite, or perlite can also be used). Wrap the cutting in a plastic bag for best results. Do this in spring or summer to ensure success. Keep it warm and in bright, but not direct, light. The lower half of the stem will not be damaged. Wrap it, pot and all, in a plastic bag. It will keep on growing and may even grow better than before. Air layering (see page 50) is the safest method of propagation for tall cuttings from one to two feet long. You can also chop a cutting into pieces three or four inches long and plant them individually either straight up or on their sides in potting soil and they will grow.

Corn Plant

(*Dracaena fragrans* and *D. fragrans massangeana*)

The corn plant is possibly the hardiest indoor tree known. It will tolerate incredible abuse. Available almost everywhere in sizes from one to five feet—and less commonly sold in sizes up to twelve feet—it is an excellent choice if you are just beginning to grow trees indoors. It will live in low light, go for long periods without water, and withstand bugs. It is truly the superplant of indoor trees. For all these reasons, and more, it is one of the trees most frequently used in offices, shopping malls, and banks.

Originally from West Africa, where it grows to twenty feet, the *Dracaena fragrans* has a tough, pale yellow, cane-like stalk topped by rosettes of fresh green to dark green leaves one to three feet long and two to four inches wide. It looks almost exactly like the massangeana, except for the color of its leaves. The massangeana has a bright yellow stripe running down the center of its leaves. It is more

Corn plant (*Dracaena fragrans*).

Corn plant (*Dracaena fragrans massangeana*). (Photo by Terrestris, N.Y.C.)

colorful than the plain fragrans and slightly more popular at the present time. Both trees have leaves which resemble the foliage of ordinary American corn plants.

If you are thinking of buying a tree-size corn plant, take your time and shop around. Prices vary greatly on tall specimens depending on where you shop. Some of the larger plant stores and discount stores are able to offer the tree at prices slightly above wholesale. Since there are so many corn plants on the market, look around until you find the handsomest and healthiest specimen at the best price. The tree is fairly slow-growing, so don't expect to buy a small plant and have it shoot up overnight into a tree.

The corn plant requires relatively little care. It will grow best in a bright spot out of direct sunlight, such as behind a light curtain or against a light wall. But it will also adapt to shadier locations and is one of the best indoor trees to use in places where other trees won't survive. If natural light is unavailable, provide the tree with artificial lighting for at least twelve hours a day.

Water the corn plant thoroughly, then allow the top of the soil to become powder-dry. Never keep the soil constantly wet. A corn plant in a twelve-inch container will need water when the top one to two inches of the soil is powder-dry.

Fertilize a small corn plant every two months, but only twice a year if full-grown. The tree will withstand temperatures down to 40 degrees, but it prefers much warmer air and does *not* need cool nights to do well. It is extremely hardy indoors because it doesn't mind the dry air of a centrally heated home.

Clean the leaves of the corn plant often to keep them glossy and free of pests. But don't worry too much about the tree being attacked by bugs.

If your corn plant gets too leggy, you can cut it down just below the foliage (or farther down the stalk) and plant the top in damp potting soil, then wrap the cutting in a plastic bag. The lower stalk will then begin to grow new leaves if you wrap it in a plastic bag, too. With tall cuttings one to two feet long, air layering (see page 50) is one safe method of propagation. To produce even more offspring, you can cut the lower stalk into pieces and plant them individually in sand-peat pots. It is sometimes possible to activate new foliage growth along a bare stalk by making a slight cut in the stalk with a knife.

The tree will thrive in the summer outdoors, but keep it in the shade and watch for pests.

Dracaena Marginata

This is one of the most graceful and intriguing-looking indoor trees we know, and also one of the hardiest. Our largest marginata is five feet tall and has grown almost a foot a year since we rescued it from a failing discount store back in 1972. We also own four more. They are as tropical-looking as palm trees, but easier to grow, and they preserve their appearance much better indoors. The marginata is becoming increasingly popular with indoor plant growers and can be found in most plant stores as a one-foot plant or specimen-size tree. In its native Africa it grows to a height of approximately fifteen feet.

The tree is easily recognized by its tall, pale, slender stem and long, silky, pointed, sword-like leaves. The leaves are colored a dark olive green and edged with red. Like a palm, its leaves grow directly from the top of its stem and notch the bark with a spiraling series of symmetrically arranged scars, so that its stem looks a little like the handle of a baseball bat bound with tape. It can be trained to grow in an amazing number of zigzagging shapes. Florida growers do this by laying the plant on its side until the stem starts twisting upward toward the light. Months later, when they place the pot back upright, the stem has developed a permanent twist. The stem will also naturally undulate as the tree matures and reaches for the light. Rotating the container at longer intervals than usual will cause the stem to twist and turn. Of course, if you want the stem to grow straight up, you should rotate the container every few weeks.

The marginata is a low-light plant and can survive on almost no sunlight at all. But if deprived of too much light, it won't increase in size. Ideally it should be kept near a window in the winter and moved a little farther back beginning in the spring. Our tallest marginata has stood in an east window for three years and done beautifully. Our smaller plants are in low-light locations such as on the mantelpiece and on top of the refrigerator! They look great where they are, but they don't grow—not more than a few inches a year. A convenient rule to follow is this: if

Madagascar dragon tree (*Dracaena marginata*). (Photo by McDonald/Mulligan)

you want to see your marginata really grow, keep it in a bright place; if you do not care how fast it grows, keep it in as dim a location as you like.

The tree will live virtually forever indoors if you water it correctly. Always let the top of the soil become powder-dry between thorough waterings. Feel the top of the soil first before you water it. If it still feels moist, move on to the next plant. When watering, soak the whole container so that all the soil gets moist. Then drain off any excess water from the drainage dish.

The marginata will automatically lose its lower leaves as it puts on new growth at the top. Don't worry if a few lower leaves turn yellow from time to time. Remove them to improve the tree's appearance. If all the leaves turn yellow, you have probably overwatered the tree. There is nothing you can do about it but cut down on the watering and pray. You might also try removing the soil mass from the pot and letting the soil dry out so the root hairs can get their long-awaited dose of oxygen.

For fast-growing, place the marginata outdoors in the shade as soon as spring arrives, but watch out for bugs, and clean the leaves more frequently. Use a timed-release fertilizer according to instructions on the label. If you use a water-soluble fertilizer, feed the tree every one to two months from early spring through fall. Only feed a tall marginata twice a year to contain its size.

The marginata will need repotting every three to five years depending on how fast it grows. Use commercial potting soil, and step up the size of the pot by an inch.

The safest way to propagate the marginata is by air layering (see page 50). Propagation by stem cutting should only be attempted in late spring or summer when the weather is warm. Cut the stem just below the foliage where the stem is still green. Apply rooting hormone powder to the cut stem. Plant the cutting in moist potting soil, vermiculite, or sand. Wrap the cutting and the pot in a plastic bag, and seal the bag shut. Place the cutting in a warm, bright location out of direct sunlight. Roots should form in two weeks to one month. The lower half of the stem will survive if you keep it in its pot and wrap it, pot and all, in a plastic bag. Within a month, it should begin to sprout a new crown. But you can also chop the stem into pieces two or three inches long and bury the pieces *lengthwise* (horizontally) in warm, damp potting soil or sand. The little cuttings will sprout. When new sprouts reach four or five inches, remove them from the parent stem *with the heel attached* and root them in damp soil.

Eucalyptus Tree

(including *Eucalyptus cinera, E. citriodora,* and *E. globulus)*

The prettiest eucalyptus tree to grow indoors is the so-called silver dollar eucalyptus, *E. cinera.* Its fragrant leaves are arranged on willowy branches like small sea shells hanging from a wind chime. When the tree reaches about six feet, its foliage changes and becomes more lance-shaped.

Unfortunately, there are more dried silver dollar leaves available than there are trees to grow indoors. One often finds the thick, durable foliage being sold for basket decorations, colored either blue-gray or rust-brown and coated with a powdery white substance that rubs off like chalk. Pot-grown silver dollar trees are scare in the north, although they are commonly sold as yard trees at garden centers in Florida and California.

Perhaps the best place to find a silver dollar plant is through a seed company. We buy our seeds from Park Seed Co., Inc., Greenwood, S.C. 29647. Silver dollar seeds are easy to grow and germinate in about five days. Sow them in ordinary moist potting soil, preferably in spring or summer, and cover the pot with plastic wrap. If you live in a warm climate where eucalypti grow outdoors, you can take a fruit from one of the trees, dry it out, and loosen the seeds inside. Plant them the same way as above. If you start the seeds indoors, the result may be a more adaptable indoor tree.

Other species of *Eucalyptus* which are sometimes grown indoors are *E. citriodora,* which has lemon-scented leaves, and *E. globulus,* commonly known as the Tasmanian blue gum. The latter grows to three hundred feet and is one of the tallest trees in the world. All three species grow fast and can reach six feet in two years with proper care.

Give eucalyptus trees full sunlight, moist soil in spring and summer, and cool fresh air in winter indoors.

Eucalyptus leaves.

When watering a tree-size eucalyptus, drench the soil and then wait until the surface becomes powder-dry. Never water the soil if it still feels moist on top. Always empty the drainage dish of excess water. A young plant in a small pot will need more frequent watering, but nevertheless, wait until the top of the soil dries out before watering. In winter, reduce the watering severely: wait about two weeks longer than normal to water the tree.

Keep the eucalyptus tree in the brightest spot in your home. Full sunlight coming from the south is ideal.

The tree does best in winter in a cool location. Night temperatures from 50 to 65 degrees are preferable. A sun porch where the temperature does not drop below 40 degrees is an excellent place to put the tree. Keep the eucalyptus away from heating units.

Eucalypti also make fine patio trees and can be shifted from the patio to the house and back again in summer if the pot is not too heavy. The tree will appreciate the cool nights and hot days.

Eucalyptus trees grown indoors are not as free-branching as in nature and should be pruned once a year to look their best. Prune two or three inches off the top of the main stem and cut the branches back slightly to shape the tree. The best time to do this is in early spring.

One word of warning: if you buy a eucalyptus at a garden center, but are thinking of growing it indoors, ease it into the lower light of your home gradually. The tree may die of shock unless you give it time to acclimatize to indoor light. Keep it outdoors under a covered porch or a heavy shade tree for the first one to two months. Then place it in the brightest window in your home. The tree will lose some of its leaves at first, but it should survive.

The fragrance of eucalyptus leaves comes from an oil known as cineole, which is used medicinally as an expectorant. It also discourages bugs from feeding on the leaves. Insects such as spider mites and white flies may occasionally bother the tree and should be sprayed off with a hose or treated with Kelthane.

False Aralia
(Dizygotheca elegantissima)

The enterprising owner of a large New York plant store recently told us that he is thinking of marketing T-shirts wildly adorned with the names of various exotic indoor plants. His favorite name is *Dizygotheca* (di-zee-go-thee′ka). "Imagine having a T-shirt with a name on it like that!" he quips.

The practically unpronounceable name of this small tree from the New Hebrides Islands in the South Pacific is Greek for "having double the usual number of anther cells." It is highly unlikely that you will ever see a false aralia bloom indoors, but at least it is comforting to know that *Dizygotheca* is not some horrible misspelling of "discothèque."

The false aralia is much easier to grow indoors when it is tall than when it's young and small. Young pot plants are prone to mealy bugs and sensitive to drafts, and they also tend to lose their lower leaves and get leggy. Tall specimens up to eight or ten feet are far more hardy indoors.

Unfortunately, it is easier to find small plants from two to four feet than it is to locate the false aralia as a full-grown tree.

The false aralia can grow a foot or more a year indoors with proper care, which means that theoretically a small plant could reach this size in five or six years. But it may look so tall and skinny by then that you will want to chop it down. In short, if you want a tree-size false aralia, the best solution is to search for a mature tree.

The average plant when young is distinguished by delicate thin leaves about four inches long radiating finger-like from the tips of dark thin branches. It usually produces from seven to eleven leaves to a cluster. The leaves are a shiny dark green, almost black, and notched along the edges. When the tree reaches six or seven feet, it suddenly begins producing leaves at least three times the size of the lacy leaves below. The upper leaves on a large specimen are some ten inches long and three inches wide.

The false aralia does best in strong indirect or filtered light, such as near a window facing south or east but behind a gauzy curtain. If natural light is unavailable, provide it with strong artificial lighting for at least twelve hours a day. In winter, it will tolerate direct sun.

Keep its soil on the dry side, giving it a good drenching and then allowing the

False aralia (*Dizygotheca elegantissima*).
(Photo by Everet Conklin Companies,
International)

top of the soil (or deeper, if it's in a large tub) to become powder-dry before watering it again. A tall false aralia in a tub twelve inches or larger should not be watered until the top two inches of the soil are powder-dry. Overwatering will kill the tree, so it is best to underwater it at the risk of losing a few leaves. Fertilize the tree every two months for average growth, every two weeks in spring and summer for maximum growth, but only two or three times a year if the tree is already specimen size.

A friend of ours has several false aralias which she grew from seed. Starting the seeds in moist potting soil and covering the small pot with plastic wrap, she found that the trees grew about three feet tall on her screened-in porch the first year. You can order the seeds from Park Seed Co., Inc., Greenwood, S.C. 29647.

The false aralia can also be propagated by rooting tip cuttings in a mixture of moist peat moss and sand.

If your tree falls prey to mealy bugs, the best cure is a systemic insecticide such as Isotox or Systemic, applied once a week for a period of three weeks. To prevent such an attack, clean the plant frequently by hosing the leaves off outside or putting the plant under the shower.

Be extra careful to keep the false aralia out of drafts. The plant likes warmth and will not live long in temperatures much below 60 degrees.

Japanese Aralia

(Fatsia japonica)

Few indoor trees have larger or more attractive foliage than the fatsia. Its stunning dark green leaves look somewhat like enormous maple leaves, although they differ with their deep and numerous lobes. The fatsia is closely related to the schefflera and rivals it for rate of growth indoors, but it is not quite as easy to grow. It will drop leaves in a room that is too warm. Keep it in a cool location in winter, and give it as much fresh air as you can.

Do not expect the fatsia to look exactly like a tree, even though it grows to six feet or more. Its foliage is so dense that the trunk is often hidden behind its leaves. The result is that it sometimes looks more like a great bush than a tree.

The fatsia needs a moderately well-lighted location out of direct sunlight or its leaves will dry up and get burned. For rapid growth, keep it just out of range of direct sunlight in a brightly lighted place. However, it will survive in a dimmer location, although not to the same extent as a dracaena or a rubber tree.

Water the fatsia thoroughly with tepid water when the surface of the soil becomes powder-dry. Never water it when the topsoil still looks dark and feels moist. Always empty the drainage dish of excess water.

Japanese aralia (*Fatsia japonica*). (Photo by Everet Conklin Companies, International)

Keep the tree away from heating units in the winter. It will grow best with temperatures between 50 and 60 degrees on winter nights. A drafty location is ideal.

For rapid growth feed the fatsia every three or four weeks in spring and summer with a water-soluble fertilizer diluted to half the recommended strength. Or use a timed-release fertilizer according to instructions on the label. Cut back the feeding in fall and winter to once every six weeks for water-soluble fertilizers. With timed-release fertilizers, feed the tree once in fall and not again until early spring. To maintain the tree at its present size, feed it only two or three times a year.

The fatsia grows fast in spring and summer (over a foot a year with proper care), and will grow even faster on a screened-in porch or in a shady place outside. Hose the leaves down regularly to discourage pests. Indoors, keep the leaves clean by sponging them with tepid water. Avoid using leaf polish products or mayonnaise to shine the leaves.

To propagate the fatsia, take stem cuttings of new leaves in spring and summer and pot them in moist potting soil. Cover the pot with plastic wrap or a plastic bag and keep it in a warm, bright location out of direct sunlight.

Ficus Trees

There are nearly eight hundred different types of trees, shrubs, and vines in the huge genus *Ficus,* among them the common fig tree. Of these, the hardy rubber tree (*Ficus elastica*) and the lovely weeping fig (*Ficus benjamina*) are by far the two most popular for indoor use. Also widely available are the Indian laurel (*F. retusa nitida*) and the gigantic fiddle-leaf fig (*F. lyrata*). In the following pages we devote separate essays to these trees (the Indian laurel is discussed in the essay on the weeping fig), but it would be a shame to overlook several other species, some of which are just as hardy indoors and often as available in plant stores.

Ficuses are second only to palms and dracaenas in terms of their hardiness, popularity, and sheer variety as indoor trees. The boom began long ago with the introduction of the rubber tree and has suddenly escalated in the last five years with the rising popularity of indoor trees. Commercial growers were perceptive enough to realize that if the rubber tree could grow so well indoors, other varieties might grow indoors as well. Today, small fortunes are being made in Florida by growers raising *Ficus* trees exclusively.

It is interesting that almost all *Ficus* trees have vine-like characteristics, even though the tree-type ficuses grow to over one hundred feet and have enormously thick trunks. In Indonesia, tall weeping figs actually entwine themselves around the trunks of even taller trees. Most ficuses also share in common a milky white sap which contains latex. While the majority of them are tropical, they belong to a family (Moraceae) which includes the mulberry tree, the Osage orange, and other trees and plants which grow in subtropical and temperate regions all over the world.

Care for *Ficus* trees differs somewhat from tree to tree, which is why we have devoted separate essays to the most popular species. Good general growing rules to follow for the trees mentioned below are:

1. *Lighting*—Avoid placing them in direct sunlight in spring and summer, but do keep them in the brightest location you can. They will all tolerate direct sunlight in winter.

2. *Watering*—Let the top of the soil become powder-dry between thorough waterings. The price of overwatering is almost certain death for these trees. Only water them when the top of the soil is dry one to two inches down. Then soak the whole pot. Always empty the drainage dish of excess water.

3. *Aerating*—Break up the top of the soil with a fork every so often to keep the soil loose and porous so that it can absorb water and air.

4. *Fresh air*—Give the trees fresh air outside in spring and summer if you can. They will grow better and will build up strength to resist the stuffy winter indoors. Place them in shade to prevent leaf burn.

5. *Feeding*—Only feed large trees once or twice a year to maintain them at their present size. Feed in early spring and late summer. Feed smaller trees every two months with a water-soluble fertilizer, or use a timed-release fertilizer following instructions on the label.

6. *Repotting*—*Ficus* trees do best in fairly small pots, so do not be too anxious to repot them. If the roots split the pot or start snaking out the drainage hole, repot them in a pot two or three inches larger using fresh potting soil. Otherwise repot every five or six years. Do not use garden loam when repotting.

7. *Pruning*—Some *Ficus* trees must be pruned at least once a year to grow well. This is true of the rubber tree, the fiddle-leaf fig, and the rusty fig. Prune two or three inches off the top of the stem of these trees in early spring. Prune other *Ficus* trees at any season to keep them looking tidy.

Some *Ficus* trees worth looking for are:

Banyan tree (*F. benghalensis*)—In India and Ceylon, the banyan is famous as a shade tree; ancient specimens develop tremendous trunks with thick aerial roots. We saw large numbers of pot-grown banyans in Florida, but whether the tree will become popular farther north, only time will tell. The banyan has attractive leath-

Banyan tree.

ery foliage, shiny and light green, three to eight inches long, and gives a durable appearance with its woody branches and sturdy main stem. Allow the top of the soil to become powder-dry between thorough waterings, and keep the tree in bright filtered or indirect light.

Common fig tree (*F. carica*)—This is the only *Ficus* tree which produces figs large enough to eat, and it will bear fruit indoors. The tree is deciduous and should get cool air and low light part of the winter in order to drop its leaves. It is infrequently sold for indoor use since it is somewhat of a challenge to grow. Beginning in November, move it to an unheated back room where the temperature is about 40 degrees but never below freezing. Keep it in low light. Reduce watering to about once a month so it can rest. The tree will drop its leaves and should be left dormant for at least sixty days. In mid-January or early February, bring it back into bright light in a warm room and gradually increase watering. The tree should bud and produce new leaves before spring. The fig tree is worth experimenting with if you have experience and really enjoy growing plants. Its large, rough foliage is not particularly attractive, but the idea of growing a real live fig tree indoors is appealing. You can try growing it indoors year-round without a dormant period, but in the long run it will not look nearly as attractive.

Common fig detail (*Ficus carica*). (Photo by T. H. Everett)

Mistletoe fig (*F. diversifolia*)—This small tree is an excellent choice if you are looking for something delicate and light. It has small, roundish, leathery leaves, about two inches long, and grows tiny yellow figs that look like mistletoe berries.

Foliage is sparse and gives the tree an airy look, somewhat like a bare branch decorated at Christmas with small lights and bulbs. It's perfect near a bright window where you want the outline of a tree but also want to let in light. From India and Indonesia, it never grows above bush size. Let the top of the soil dry out between thorough waterings.

Mistletoe fig (*Ficus diversifolia*) detail. (Photo by T. H. Everett)

Mistletoe fig (*Ficus diversifolia*). (Photo by T. H. Everett)

Religiosa (*F. religiosa*)—The bo tree is said to be the tree under which Buddha received enlightenment nearly five hundred years before Christ. It is considered sacred in India, where it grows to a huge and glorious old age. The tree has beautiful blue-gray, heart-shaped leaves with prominent yellow-green veins and a delicate drip tip curling off at the end of each leaf. Often planted outdoors in Florida, it is only occasionally available in plant stores. Like other ficuses, it should be kept in bright filtered or indirect light and should not be watered until the top of the soil becomes powder-dry.

Religiosa fig (*Ficus religiosa*).

Rusty fig (*F. rubiginosa*)—For sheer good looks, this is one of our favorite indoor trees, but it can be difficult to grow. From Australia, it has small, leathery, rounded leaves, dark green in color verging on black. The foliage looks very much like a scaled-down version of the leaves on a rubber tree. New leaves unfold out of slender green spikes exactly like rubber tree leaves. While some of its features remind us of a rubber tree, it is really much more delicate and better-looking. The trunk is brown, woody, and erect. It is commonly called rusty fig for the rust-red spots which sometimes appear on its leaves. Water this tree as you would a rubber tree, always letting the top of the soil dry out between drenchings, but keep it in strong indirect or filtered light. Give it cool night temperatures in winter. Prune the top two to three inches off the main stem to stimulate branching.

Triangle-leafed fig (*F. triangularis*)—This interesting tree has small, thick, triangular leaves, one to two inches long on all three sides, and is fairly common in plant stores. Its geometrical foliage is unusual and quite attractive, but we have not seen any specimens with really sturdy stems. In plain English, the tree tends to be skinny and leggy. Keep it in bright indirect or curtain-filtered light and water it thoroughly when the top of the soil becomes powder-dry.

Rusty fig (*Ficus rubiginosa*).

Triangle-leafed fig (*Ficus triangularis*).

Fiddle-leaf Fig

(Ficus lyrata, also called Ficus pandurata)

The monstrous leaves of this tropical West African tree are shaped like a fiddle and grow one to two feet long. Indoors the tree is incredibly bulky and requires a great deal of space. The leaves grow directly from growth spikes on the brown, woody main stem like the leaves of a rubber tree. Outdoors the fiddle-leaf fig can reach forty feet.

While the tree is often mentioned in books on indoor plants, few writers bother to point out that it can look hideous unless it is properly grown. As its leaves grow older and larger, they turn dry and hard. They get brown at the edges if you over-water or underwater the soil. Radical shifts of temperature can also damage the leaves. In short, while the tree may survive a long time, the chances are that it will get progressively worse-looking unless you give it proper care.

The first thing to realize is that the tree will continue to grow straight up and look spindly unless you keep it pruned. Clip off the top two or three inches of the

Fiddle-leaf fig (*Ficus lyrata*).

Fiddle-leaf fig detail (*Ficus lyrata*).

main stem once or twice a year for best results. Radical as this may seem, the procedure will force the tree to produce new leaves and branches farther down the stem. If you do not prune it, the spaces between the leaves will increase to the point where the tree will look like a lopsided broomstick.

Equally important is how you water the tree. Overwatering will turn the edges of the leaves brown and in time the roots will rot. Underwatering will also brown the edges of the leaves. This is one tropical tree that really requires even watering. The best method is to water it thoroughly—soak the whole pot—and then wait until the top of the soil becomes powder-dry. Check the pot every four or five days to see how the soil looks and feels. Don't water it until the soil turns gray and feels like ash on top. On the other hand, don't leave it ashy very long. After you have owned the tree for a few months, you should be able to tell what kind of a watering schedule it needs. Then stick to the schedule.

Keep the tree in bright curtain-filtered light or in bright indirect light against a light wall. Avoid direct sunlight, especially from the south, but do keep the tree in a bright place.

The fiddle-leaf fig is temperamental when it comes to temperature. Keep it in a warm room out of drafts and avoid radical shifts from hot to cold. A low of 60 degrees at night won't hurt the tree, but don't expose it to much cooler air.

For rapid growth, feed the tree with a timed-release fertilizer following the instructions on the label. For slower growth, apply a water-soluble plant food once or twice a year. The tree is relatively fast-growing and can increase a foot or more a year if it spends the spring and summer outdoors in the shade.

Repot the fiddle-leaf fig in commercial potting soil, stepping up the size of the pot by one or two inches every four or five years.

Rubber Tree
(Ficus elastica)

Many a fledgling rubber tree owner has suffered a shattering loss of self-esteem upon watching—and sometimes even hearing—his first rubber tree die.

When the tree is dying, you can sometimes hear its huge leaves hit the floor in the middle of the night. They fall with a loud dry clack. The sound is infinitely more melancholy than the rustling of autumn leaves. If you are suffering from a sense of inadequacy already, the death of a rubber tree could easily drive you mad.

The fact is that the rubber tree is a deceiving plant. It looks so strong and healthy standing there erect and green in its pot in the shop. But it is easy to kill until you get the feel of it. And the key to getting the feel of it lies in the art of *watering*.

The temptation most novices have is to water their rubber tree every two or three days. Don't! *We only water ours once every two weeks.* It is true that our two trees are planted in large, ten-inch plastic pots, and that the pots do not have drainage holes, so that their soil takes longer to dry out. But even if yours is growing in a porous clay pot and draining water out the bottom freely, it is still imperative not to overwater it. Always let the top of the soil become powder-dry between waterings.

The reason the rubber tree does not need frequent watering is because of its large, tough, waxy leaves. The leaves store water like a camel's hump. Too much water will simply bloat the tree and rot the roots. Before you know it your floor will be littered with huge dead leaves.

We pour approximately one third of a gallon of tepid water into the soil of each of our trees once every two weeks and leave it at that. Between April and October, we also fertilize them once a month with a liquid plant food. During fall and winter we cut the fertilizing back to once every two months.

The other key to keeping your rubber tree alive is to place it in a spot out of direct sunlight. Its leaves scorch easily. Ours have been growing for four years in our dining room, which faces west and gets little direct sunlight in the summer due to several overgrown hedges and a large elm tree outside. In the winter, the room is fairly bright, but it rarely gets direct sun.

Once you learn that the rubber tree does not like frequent watering or blazing sun, you can begin to tell your friends that it is practically impossible to kill. Along with our scheffleras and dracaena marginatas, our rubber trees are among our sturdiest and fastest-growing plants. They may seem like humdrum houseplants that have been around for years, but at least one reason for their popularity is that they satisfy the indoor gardener's urge to watch things grow. It is amazing how frequently they produce new leaves, like soft green shiny babies, fresh and tender-skinned beside the old, thick, dark green, hard adults.

Pruning is especially important with the rubber tree, since it tends to grow

Rubber tree (*Ficus elastica*).

straight up and get spindly. To avoid this, clip off the top two or three inches of the plant once a year. Follow the same procedure with the tips of branches. Pruning will help the tree produce new leaves and branches farther down the stem. If you buy a small rubber tree with a single stem and no branches, prune the top off as soon as you bring it home. Within six months it will start to branch.

The rubber tree will thrive in the summer outdoors. But keep it in the shade. Also be careful that it doesn't tip over in a thunderstorm or get pelted by hail, as ours once did, or you'll find yourself with rubber tree leaves riddled with cuts and holes that can never be repaired.

The best way to prevent a bug attack is to keep the leaves clean. Wash them with a very mild solution of Ivory soap and tepid water on both sides of the leaves. Then wipe the soap off with a damp cloth.

In its native Malaya, and even not-so-native Florida, the rubber tree grows to a fantastic height. Indoors, it may eventually grow too large for you. To keep the tree in line, simply trim it to the size you want, or air-layer it (see page 50) and start a second tree, or take stem cuttings about four inches down new green growing tips and propagate the clippings in moist potting soil or builder's sand, wrapping the cuttings in a plastic bag. The rubber tree, which was once used as a source for rubber but was replaced by the *Hevea brasiliensis* and then synthetics, has long· been known as an ideal subject to practice your first air-layering experiments upon.

There is a variegated variety of the rubber tree called *Ficus elastica* 'Doescheri' which is not nearly as common in plant stores as the normal elastica.

Weeping Fig
(Ficus benjamina)

The weeping fig is that rarest of all things, an indoor tree that really *looks* like a tree. It is tremendously popular today because it does not look the least bit tropical and because it holds up very well indoors. In fact, the demand for it is so great that in some areas of the country it is becoming hard to find.

The weeping fig comes from Indonesia and grows to over one hundred feet outdoors. Its small, shiny, fresh green leaves often remind us of the leaves on the pear tree in our own back yard. The trunk of the weeping fig is smooth and silver-gray and looks somewhat like the trunk of a birch. Its graceful branches droop slightly like the branches of a weeping willow. Both the weeping fig and its close relatives *Ficus exotica* and *Ficus philippinense* are stunning trees which the indoor grower will find hard to resist. Another popular *Ficus* tree is the Indian laurel or *F. retusa nitida,* which is often trained as a handsome standard. From a distance, the weeping fig and the Indian laurel appear similar, but their leaves are different. The Indian laurel's are broader, flatter, and thicker. The benjamina's are more delicate.

Beauty has its price, and unfortunately all four of these trees are expensive ($35 and up for a four-to-six-foot tree). However, you can cut corners and buy smaller specimens for less and then enjoy watching them grow into trees. They will grow

Weeping fig (*Ficus benjamina*).

Leaves of *Ficus benjamina*.

Leaves of Indian laurel (*Ficus retusa nitida*).

as much as a foot a year outside in the shade in spring and summer. Full-grown specimens can be maintained at their present size by keeping the fertilizing down to once or twice a year and by occasionally pruning the tree to keep it in line.

Since you will invest $20 at the very least in one of these trees, you should be especially careful to water it correctly and provide the right light. How you water the tree (any indoor tree) is the most important thing.

It is essential that you *never* water a weeping fig until the top of the soil becomes powder-dry. Do not hover over it and water it every day, thinking you can somehow speed up its growth. It will die if you do. Check the soil every four or five days to see how it looks. When the top of the soil feels dry, water it thoroughly with tepid water. Pour enough water in to soak the whole container. Then let the water drain off and and empty the dish in which the container stands. Always resist the impulse to water the tree if the top of the soil looks dark and still feels moist. Too much concern for the tree will inevitably lead to overwatering, overfeeding, overpotting—in short, excess in all the wrong things.

Finding the best light situation is also important. All three of these ficuses are gluttons for light, so the more light the better. Do not put them in direct sunlight, in spring or summer, but do keep them in the most intense curtain-filtered or indirect light in your home. Too much shade and their leaves will all drop off. During the winter months they will tolerate direct sunlight at any exposure in your home. You may even want to supplement the natural light by using an incandescent floodlight at a range of three or four feet for five or six hours a day. If you choose a spot for the tree where natural light is not abundant, then extend the hours of artificial illumination so that your tree is receiving a total of sixteen hours of light daily.

A troublesome feature of these trees is that they tend to defoliate, sometimes severely, when they are first brought home. The trees may be shedding old leaves which were adapted to strong sunlight and are in the process of growing new leaves adapted to shade. These shade-grown leaves are structurally different from sun-grown leaves. They tend to be larger, flatter, and thinner in order to soak up all available light. Sun-grown leaves are comparatively small, thick, and curled. The thickness is to prevent the interior of the leaves from getting burned. The curl or V-shape of the leaves is another defense against strong sun, and it also serves as a convenient trough for catching rain. The leaves are smaller than shade-grown leaves simply because they don't need so much surface area to catch the sun. If you buy a benjamina or an Indian laurel and it defoliates when you first bring it home, don't panic. Put it in the brightest window in your home, or leave it outdoors for a month or two in the shade. Misting its leaves daily will also help a great deal.

The problem of leaf drop has its advantages in the long run. A sun-grown benjamina is not nearly as lovely as one grown in shade. It is thick and bushy. The delicate structure of the trunk and branches doesn't show through. As the leaves fall off, the tree takes on the gracefulness of a birch or of a weeping willow in a Japanese print. It is worth being suspicious if you see a bushy benjamina or Indian laurel in a plant store. The tree may have just arrived from Florida and never acclimatized to shade. Look for a tree with a moderate amount of leaves where the structure of the branches shows through.

The trees grow best when continued in fairly small pots. You will only need to repot them every four or five years. Use ordinary commercial potting soil and increase pot size by no more than one inch.

Do not fertilize any of these trees for the first six months. Then feed them with a water-soluble plant food every two months or use a timed-release fertilizer according to the instructions on the label.

The trees will tolerate average house temperatures, but they thrive in an atmosphere that is pleasantly moist. Give their leaves a good misting every day in winter. If the air is allowed to become excessively dry, there is the risk of red spider mites attacking the leaves. The foliage then becomes flecked with a kind of yellow dust and, in extreme cases, a white cottony web will appear on the underside of the leaves. The best preventive is to keep the leaves well wiped, but if such an attack does occur, treat the leaves with Kelthane until cured.

Giant Dumb Cane
(Dieffenbachia amoena)

This huge, fast-growing plant has been popular with indoor gardeners for well over a hundred years. It has massive and unmistakable variegated green and creamy-white leaves. Commonly called dumb cane because its erect green stalk resembles cane—and because it secretes a poison called calcium oxalate which can render you speechless for a day or two if you suck too much juice from the foliage or the stalk—the plant is extremely hardy and requires little care.

From Colombia, the giant dumb cane is the largest of over fifty species of *Dieffenbachia* in cultivation. It can grow to over six feet high indoors. A small plant will reach that size in two or three years if given fresh air outdoors in spring and summer or grown on a screened-in porch. Kept indoors permanently in low light, it will of course take longer to grow.

Dieffenbachias tolerate fairly low light and are therefore useful in dim places where many trees and houseplants won't survive. The dimmer the light, however, the slower the plant will grow. For rapid growth, it will thrive in diffused sunlight,

Giant dumb cane (*Dieffenbachia amoena*). (Photo by Everet Conklin Companies, International)

such as behind a thin light curtain, or in bright indirect light near a light wall. But full sun may wilt the plant and burn its leaves.

The dumb cane likes moderately dry soil. Water it thoroughly with tepid water, then wait until the top of the soil is powder-dry before watering it again. Never water it when the surface of the soil is still moist.

For rapid growth, fertilize the plant with a timed-release fertilizer according to instructions on the label. Or use a water-soluble fertilizer diluted to half the recommended strength every two to three months.

The one thing the dumb cane will not tolerate is cold. Keep it out of drafts. It should always be kept in a place where the temperature does not drop below 60 degrees.

Because the plant grows fast, it may need repotting as often as once a year. Use commercial potting soil and step up the size of the container by two or three inches.

Dieffenbachias are easy to propagate, and there may come a time when you will want to do so if the plant gets too tall. Several methods of propagation will work. Tall cuttings one to two feet long should be propagated by air layering (see page 50) or by planting the cutting in moist potting soil and sealing it in a clear plastic bag. Shorter cuttings can be grown in a glass of water and planted in potting soil when a good root system has formed. They can also be planted directly into potting soil, perlite, or vermiculite and covered with a plastic bag. Do not throw away the lower stalk; it will sprout new leaves. Another method of propagation is to chop a cutting into pieces three to five inches long. Lay the pieces horizontally on a bed of damp potting soil, and they will sprout.

Among the smaller species of *Dieffenbachia* available are *D. picta*, *D. picta* 'Rudolph Roehrs,' which is very attractive, and *D. exotica*. Any one of these plants will live indoors for years with proper care. But the giant dumb cane will give you the greatest satisfaction if you want a tree-size plant.

Hawaiian Ti Plant
(Cordyline terminalis)

This colorful plant or small tree is often found in tropical plant stores in the form of a two-inch "log" wrapped in sphagnum moss and packaged in a small plastic bag. It can also be ordered by mail through advertisements in many house and garden magazines, and established plants are easy to find in sizes from one to three feet. When planted in a pot and given water, the log sprouts and develops striking reddish-pink and dark green leaves. Over the course of several years, it will begin to grow a pale, slender, erect stem similar to that of a *Dracaena marginata,* to which it is closely related.

Long before it decorated American homes, the ti plant was used in Hawaii and on other Polynesian islands to thatch huts and make hula skirts. Its normal height is about ten feet, although one variety from New Zealand called mountain cabbage (*Cordyline indivisa*) grows forty feet high or more. The most commonly sold vari-

Ti plant (*Cordyline terminalis*). (Photo by Genereux Library)

ety is the red and green *C. terminalis* 'Bicolor,' but there is also a 'Tricolor' variety with red, green, and white leaves. The red color in the leaves of all these trees is reminiscent of the color of red cabbage.

Ti plants are extremely easy to propagate, which is why they are so often sold as "logs." The packaged log is simply a piece of cane chopped off the stem of a large plant and coated with wax. It may look old and dry wrapped up in all that stringy moss, but success in making it grow is virtually guaranteed. All you have to do is plant the log and the moss in a pot, give it water, and wait for it to grow. Whether you can keep the young plant alive long enough to grow a tree depends on whether you water it correctly and give it the right light, but the most important factor is whether it gets enough humidity in winter to keep its leaves from drying out.

To increase humidity around the plant in winter, the best method is to put the pot in a shallow pan or tray filled with pebbles and water. Set the pot on top of the stones, and make sure the water level does not reach the bottom of the pot and soak the soil through the drainage holes. It is also wise to group the ti plant near other foliage plants and to give it a daily misting. The best location for the plant is of course a greenhouse, if you happen to have one in your home.

Keep the ti plant out of hot, direct sunlight in spring and summer to protect its leaves, but always grow it in bright light. It will tolerate sunlight in the winter.

As a "log," the soil of the ti plant will need to be kept constantly moist. But as it matures into an established plant and then into a tree, it should only be watered when the top of the soil becomes powder-dry. Other books on indoor gardening may tell you to keep its soil moist, but this does not mean watering it every day. It means that you should water it well and then wait until the top of the soil dries out and becomes gray. Constantly dark topsoil means that you are overwatering the plant and not giving it a chance to breathe.

For rapid growth, feed the ti plant every one to two months with a water-soluble plant food or use a timed-release fertilizer following the instructions on the label. Put the plant outside or on a screened-in porch as soon as spring arrives, but always keep it in a shady location where direct sunlight does not reach it until late in the day. The most effective way to grow a ti plant fast is to plunge it in its pot in the garden. But, again, you will have to find a shady garden spot to keep its leaves from burning up.

The ti plant is fairly slow-growing and will take two or three years to develop a tree-like stem if you start it as a log. If it eventually grows too tall or leggy, you can chop it into pieces and start new plants from your own home-grown logs. Use ordinary commercial potting soil both when propagating and repotting.

Jade Tree
(Crassula argentea)

At a cactus farm in Florida last year, we saw a huge shipment of jade trees which had just arrived from Japan. The eight-inch plants had been wrapped in Japanese newspaper and shipped without soil. Their bare roots were long, white, and dry. A sizable group of women was standing on either side of a long workbench busily potting the plants.

Needless to say, considering the way they were shipped, the length of the journey they had made, and the rough treatment they received as the women plunged them into pots, the jade plants had to be a hardy lot to survive.

Originally from South Africa, but associated with Japan now and the art of bonsai, the jade is characterized by small, thick, oval, jade-green leaves one to two inches long growing on tree-like branches from an unusually thick trunk. When looked at closely, it is among the most amazing indoor trees—a kind of instant bonsai.

Jades are sold as seedlings in small pots or as delightful miniature trees from one to three feet. A three-foot jade can be expensive ($40 or more), but if you want one that really looks like a tree, the investment is worth it. Since the plant is extremely slow-growing, a small jade may tax your patience. Over the course of a decade, a two-foot specimen may grow to four feet. In their native habitat they sometimes reach ten feet. To achieve a full bonsai effect with a jade and really make it look like a tree, you should clip the lower branches to accentuate the trunk and prune upper branches and leaves to reveal the structure of the main limbs.

The jade is virtually indestructible if grown with proper care. The name *Crassula* derives from the Latin *crassus,* meaning "thick" or "fleshy," and while the jade is far from a crass-looking plant, it does have a thick skin and will survive a long time. The tree thrives on direct sunlight, cool night temperatures, and moderately dry soil.

For best results, put the tree in full sun at a south window. It will also grow in

Jade tree (*Crassula argentea*). (Photo by Terrestris, N.Y.C.)

bright filtered light or in bright indirect light against a white wall. If grown under artificial light, it should receive at least twelve hours a day under a 150-watt bulb placed two feet above the tree. During its resting period in fall and winter, it can go for longer periods in lower light. But continual low-light conditions will cause its leaves to yellow and drop off, and eventually the plant will die.

The thick succulent leaves of the jade are efficient reservoirs, enabling the plant to live without water for a considerable length of time. It is best, however, to water the jade thoroughly and then allow the top inch of the soil to dry out before watering it again. The one thing the tree will not tolerate is overwatering and soggy soil. Never let the plant stand in water.

A small jade will need repotting about once a year; larger specimens should be left in the same container for about four years. Use commercial potting soil mixed with sand when potting.

Fertilize the tree once every three or four months.

The jade will withstand temperatures between 40 and 100 degrees and does best when night temperatures drop to 50 or 60 degrees on fall and winter nights.

The tree can be propagated by rooting tip cuttings in potting soil or in a glass of water. Individual leaves planted base down in potting soil will also take.

The jade produces lovely pink flowers if you leave it outside all spring, but it rarely blooms indoors.

Japanese Pittosporum or Australian Laurel

(Pittosporum tobira)

One of the common names for this tough shrub from Japan and China is incongruously "Australian laurel." The name comes from the fact that most species of *Pittosporum* live in Australia—even though the *tobira* does not—and also from the fact that its leathery leaves resemble laurel leaves. It is usually sold as a two-to-three-foot shrub with thin woody stems and shiny, dark green, oblong leaves. There is also a variegated pittosporum with gray-green leaves and cream-colored margins. The leaves of both these species are two to four inches long and tend to curl downward at the edges, sometimes forming a kind of tube. For some reason they remind us of cinnamon sticks. The foliage is so tough that it makes a clacking sound when you shake the plant.

Pittosporums can grow to nine or ten feet, but specimens that size are unavailable in stores. Shrubs three to four feet high are more common and make handsome tub plants in entrance halls or outside by the front door. They love cool weather and can stay outside into early fall before night temperatures drop below freezing.

Japanese pittosporum (*Pittosporum tobira*). (Photo by T. H. Everett)

Pittosporum tobira detail. (Photo by T. H. Everett)

For best results, grow the pittosporum in full sun or in bright light against a light wall. It will adapt to lower light, although it will not grow as actively under such conditions and may not look as good. A specimen grown in good strong light may bloom in the spring with small white flowers scented like orange blossoms. But don't expect it to bloom in lower light.

Water the pittosporum thoroughly, then allow the top one to two inches of the soil to become powder-dry before watering it thoroughly again. In a container twelve inches or larger, wait until the soil is dry one to two inches down. Like a rubber tree, it prefers to be drenched and then allowed to become fairly dry. Its waxy leaves do not transpire as fast as the leaves of many plants.

Since the plant favors cool air, it will grow beautifully with night temperatures between 40 and 60 degrees. Either a cool, drafty entranceway or a sun porch where the temperature does not drop below freezing is ideal. The pittosporum may look sickly in a room with stuffy air and will be easy prey for spider mites. To discourage pests, mist and clean the leaves frequently in winter.

Fertilize a mature pittosporum twice a year in very early spring and early summer; younger plants can be fertilized every two months, but do not feed them in winter.

The shrub grows slowly and can live for a long time in the same pot. Use commercial potting soil when repotting every four or five years.

Propagation is by seed, air layering (see page 50), or stem cutting. Take stem cuttings in midsummer, clipping stems four to five inches down new green growing tips. Plant them in damp potting soil and cover with plastic wrap. It is best to treat them with rooting powder before you do so.

Jasmine
(Jasminum grandiflorum)

While most jasmines are ordinarily grown in small pots for the delicious fragrance of their flowers, some species can look extremely attractive indoors as mature shrubs three to four feet tall. They have beautiful, delicate, dark green, tear-shaped leaves, similar in shape and size to the leaves of a locust tree. Their branches are thin, woody, hedge-like, and erect. A tall jasmine is a refreshing change from a rubber tree or a schefflera, since it looks so light, non-tropical, and cool. The only trouble is that jasmines can be tricky to grow, and shrub-size jasmines are definitely hard to find. We discovered the four-foot specimen in the photograph at a plant store in Connecticut, but it was the first large pot-grown jasmine we had ever seen.

Of the many species of jasmine available, the best to grow as a shrub is the *grandiflorum,* Spanish jasmine.

All jasmines have white, star-shaped flowers with a fragrance so enticing that it

Jasmine (*Jasminum grandiflorum*).

is bottled in perfumes and celebrated in poems and songs. While jasmine is usually associated with Persia and Arabia, it also grows in India, China, and the South Pacific. Like its relatives *Forsythia* and lilac, it belongs to the large, sweet-smelling olive family.

For best results, grow jasmine in full sunlight in the winter, then switch it to bright filtered light during the summer. Habitual jasmine growers like to put their plants outside in the spring and keep them out all summer. A tall jasmine in a tub makes an ideal patio plant.

Keep the soil of the jasmine constantly moist during the warm months, watering it as soon as the surface of the soil dries out, but not before. Drench the whole pot and empty the drainage dish of excess water. In fall and winter, put the plant in a cool, dim location where the temperature is between 50 and 60 degrees. Water the soil about once a month. In late January, bring the plant out into full sun and commence regular watering.

Feed the plant with a water-soluble fertilizer diluted to half the recommended strength every two to four weeks in spring and summer. Do not fertilize it during the fall and winter.

A shrub-size jasmine will need frequent pruning if you want a shapely plant. Prune it in early fall and then again in late spring or early summer to control new growth.

Propagate jasmine by planting green stem cuttings in moist potting soil in spring or summer. Cover the pot with plastic wrap or a plastic bag.

Jerusalem Cherry Tree
(Solanum pseudo-capsicum)

No indoor plant or small tree has given us more satisfaction over the years than our Jerusalem cherry trees. They are extremely hardy, easy to propagate, and fun to have around. When they blossom and bear red, cherry-tomato-like fruit, they are the loveliest plants in our home.

Whatever you do, don't throw a Jerusalem cherry tree away—even if it looks dead. The tree has amazing powers of recuperation. The plant will live and bear fruit indoors for years. Eventually it will grow into a small, tough-stemmed tree. You can prune the lower branches to create a more tree-like effect, or you can let it grow into a full, wild bush. If you enjoy bonsai, you should seriously consider the Jerusalem cherry as a candidate, even though it is not traditionally known as a bonsai tree.

At the last count, we owned eight Jerusalem cherry trees. We sold several dozen more at yard sales or gave them away. Our first tree came from the fruit of a huge Jerusalem cherry that was grown by a tiny Mexican Indian lady named Tata. Tata's tree grew outside in a bucket on the front steps of an estate in Virginia. Last year, the family that she worked for moved to Mexico temporarily, taking Tata with them, much to our distress. When Tata moved away, she left her huge Jerusalem cherry tree locked inside the house. Eight months later, when she re-

Jerusalem cherry (*Solanum pseudo-capsicum*). (Photo by T. H. Everett)

turned, the tree, of course, was dead . . . Or was it? Tata mixed some fresh manure in the soil, cut the branches back, and put the tree back out on the front
steps. A month later it was a beautiful green tree again, flowering and bearing fruit.

The formula for growing a Jerusalem cherry tree is simple: it needs full sunlight
and lots of water. Our largest tree is still growing in soil we dug up behind the
horse barn out on the estate where Tata lives. The soil has manure in it, but it
tends to dry out much too fast and gets too hard, so we recommend that you grow
yours in ordinary commercial potting soil. Even then, the tree has a tremendous
thirst. The leaves will let you know when they need water, since they wilt exactly
like the leaves of a young tomato plant. But they spring back within an hour with a
fresh dose of tepid water.

We fertilize our trees once a month year-round with either a water-soluble plant
food or Plant Tabs.

The Jerusalem cherry is among the easiest indoor trees to propagate. Simply sink
one of the ripened fruits in a small pot, about half an inch below the soil (ordinary
potting soil is fine), water thoroughly, cover the pot with plastic wrap, and wait a
month or a month and a half for the seedlings to appear. A shriveled fruit will also
work. We usually start our seedlings in early spring, several fruits to a pot, and
then in late spring remove them from the pot and plant them straight into the garden. By early October they have grown eight inches and can be transplanted back
into individual pots and brought inside. A Jerusalem cherry tree makes a nice gift.
But warn your friends that the fruit is mildly poisonous.

Historically speaking, the Jerusalem cherry is a venerable plant, having been
grown indoors in Europe since at least the 1600s. The famous horticulturist L. H.

Bailey has a fascinating chapter on the origin of its name in his classic book *How Plants Get Their Names*. According to Bailey the plant does not come from Jerusalem and may even grow worldwide. A visitor to Jerusalem must have chanced upon some seeds there and brought them back to Europe, thinking that the plant was native to Jerusalem, and so called it a Jerusalem cherry when he saw the cherry-like fruit. The plant is a member of the potato family (Solanaceae) and bears a strong resemblance to its cousin the red pepper (*Capsicum*), and so is called a false capsicum.

The greatest peril to the health of the Jerusalem cherry is the white fly, which invades the tree by the millions when it strikes. This is the price you may have to pay for putting your tree outside. We have done only a fair job of controlling this infuriating pest by hosing the tree down outside. If things get really bad, you should spray the tree with Isotox or feed it a systemic insecticide, three weeks in succession once each week. But there is no guarantee that even an atomic bomb will exterminate this fast-breeding, leaf-sucking little fly.

Loquat Tree or Japanese Plum
(Eriobotrya japonica)

We own a loquat tree, but, alas, our luck with it has not been very good. It bears almost no resemblance to the shapely loquat pictured. As we write these lines, it is standing out on the back lawn in an old pail. It has a stump for a trunk that we sawed off when its main stem died. Out of this stump grow two skinny branches topped by a few old leaves. The leaves are rough, dark green, sawtoothed at the edges, crinkly to the touch, and covered with white fuzz. The fuzz looks somewhat like dust. The tree belongs to the genus *Eriobotrya*, which is Greek for "woolly cluster." The name is a fairly accurate description of the white, woolly fuzz which coats its clusters of new leaves.

We thought that we were getting a good deal on our tree when we bought it. A chain of discount stores was on the verge of going bankrupt. The outlet nearest us had resorted to stocking an incredible assortment of tropical plants, along with Indian shirts and beads, hoping to pick up sales. The ploy didn't work. When the chain went bankrupt, the prices on the plants came tumbling down. We descended on the place like two piranhas. Half the plants and trees that we now own we bought there. The loquat was our only casualty.

This is the risk you take when you buy your plants and trees in a discount store. But considering the money you can save, you really can't complain when one or two of the plants fail. In the long run, it is worth doing at least some of your plant shopping in such a place.

We have yet to see a really gorgeous loquat tree growing indoors. Like ours, they tend to be skinny-stemmed and skimpy-leaved. If you want to add a loquat tree to your collection, we suggest that you invest some money and buy a handsome, full-grown specimen like the one in the picture. Don't try cutting corners like us.

Loquat tree (*Eriobotrya japonica*).   Loquat leaves detail.

The best place to put your tree, so that it won't become like ours, is in good, strong, direct sunlight. It likes fresh air, so try to keep it near an open window in the summer. The tree is tough and drought-resistant. You should drench it and then always let the top one to two inches of the soil dry out. In winter, it prefers a cool location, and watering then should be considerably reduced. A good rule to follow for winter watering is: if it seems to be ready for water (the way you would water it in spring and summer), then wait an extra two weeks before you drench it.

If you own a nice, full tree, keep the fertilizing down to twice a year. Otherwise the tree may grow too fast and lose its shape. It won't hurt the leaves to wipe their woolly coating off. But restrain yourself until the leaves have grown mature.

Of all our indoor plants and trees, the loquat seems to do the best outdoors. Its tough leaves can withstand wind, rain, and hail. Bugs can be a problem, so keep the leaves well washed. In any case, the loquat tree has always been more popular in the yard than indoors. It grows outside in Florida, California, and throughout the Gulf States, withstanding temperatures down to 10 degrees. For best results, give it cool night air in winter, preferably below 65 degrees. The tree seldom bears fruit north of citrus country, and we have never heard of any loquat bearing fruit indoors. The fruit grows either round or pear-shaped, tastes somewhat like a cherry, and is about the size of a plum.

Our loquat seemed to die shortly after we bought it. We put it outside behind the garage, without a leaf on it, and within a month it came back to life. If you have any indoor tree with a *woody* stem that seems to be dead, don't give up on it too fast. Put it outside for the summer. If it hasn't grown a leaf by fall, chop it up and use it for kindling. At least it will have served some purpose in life.

Meanwhile, our own loquat is threatening to revive again. Above those ancient, wrinkled leaves are sprouting woolly clusters of new growth. Small pale leaves are even sprouting from the base of the sawed-off trunk. We keep meaning to air-layer the sturdier of the two branches and start from scratch, plant it down in some fresh soil and see how it grows. But propagating trees takes love, and to date our loquat tree has strained our love. We certainly wish you better luck with yours.

Ming Tree and Balfour Aralia
(Polyscias fruticosa, P. balfouriana)

The ming tree is justly famous for its gnarled, craggy, ancient-looking trunk and small, delicate, jagged-edged leaves. Although it comes from Malaysia, it looks straight out of a Chinese or Japanese print. The tree can be grown to seven or eight feet indoors, but it also makes an ideal bonsai. To us, the ming almost instantly conjures up visions of an old Victorian parlor with dark oak paneling, dim stained glass windows, china bulldogs by the fireplace, and oriental rugs on the floor. Sitting on a long, heavy table behind the couch, in a precious china pot, is an old neglected ming tree with a few discolored, ragged leaves.

The reason that we envision the tree as having so few leaves is that the parlor is so dimly lit. The ming is a high-light tree and requires direct sunlight, bright diffuse light, or bright indirect light against a light wall. It may survive indefinitely in lower light, but it will lose most of its leaves.

The same rule applies to the Balfour aralia, which is closely related to the ming but has round, green, gardenia-like leaves two to four inches wide and a trunk which is usually more erect and skinnier than the ming's.

Both these trees—as well as numerous other species of *Polyscias*—require basically the same care. Along with bright light, they like soil on the dry side. Water them thoroughly, then allow the top of the soil to become powder-dry before watering them thoroughly again. The trees like warmth and should be kept out of drafts in a room where the temperature does not drop below 65 degrees. They thrive in high humidity. For best results, place them near other foliage plants in the winter or in trays filled with pebbles and water. Also mist the leaves as often as you can. Fertilize them every three to four months year-round.

The ming tree is sometimes called a "nervous plant" because it tends to defoliate when moved around. But in most cases the tree springs back and grows *lusher* foliage after such a setback.

Both of these trees are extremely slow-growing, so do not expect to see an eight-inch pot plant suddenly shoot up into a six-foot tree. Large specimens which look centuries old are usually grown from cuttings off an old tree. For instance, an ancient-looking four-foot ming selling for $60 is probably a five-year-old cutting off an eighty- or ninety-year-old tree. Many plant stores carry at least one or two of these "old" trees.

If you want an indoor tree that will live almost indefinitely, either of these species is an excellent investment. Both the ming and the Balfour aralia are among the

Ming tree (*Polyscias fruiticosa*).

Balfour aralia (*P. balfouriana*). (Photo by Terrestris, N.Y.C.)

hardiest of all the indoor trees. Other species of *Polyscias* available are *P. fruticosa elegans,* a smaller and more delicate ming with parsley-like leaves; *P. guilfoylei quinquefolia,* commonly called celery-leaved panax, which has large shiny oak-like leaves and makes a very handsome foliage plant; *P. balfouriana marginata,* a variegated version of the Balfour aralia; and *P. balfouriana pennockii,* or white aralia, with creamy-white leaves. An intriguing variety of Balfour aralia is the so-called "dinner plate aralia" with lily-pad-like leaves six to eight inches across.

Monkey-puzzle Tree
(*Araucaria bidwillii* and *A. araucana*)

The Norfolk Island pine is the most popular of the *Araucaria* trees, but there are two others, called monkey-puzzle trees, which you might find interesting. One of these, the *bidwillii,* is easy to find in plant stores and may one day surpass the Norfolk Island pine in popularity. It is just as hardy, if not hardier, than the Norfolk Island pine.

Native to Australia, the *bidwillii* has small, vicious, prickly leaves and odd, disjointed branches. While it is not as handsome as the Norfolk Island pine, it makes an interesting, if uncomfortable, conversation piece. Watch out: it scratches and can rip your clothes and is not ideal if you have children. The tree is definitely out for blood.

The other monkey-puzzle tree, *araucana,* is from Chile and has stiff, leathery, pointed needles growing close to the branch. Its branches are even odder and more disjointed than the *bidwillii*'s. The tree is unusually hardy outdoors and was popular in nineteenth-century Great Britain, where it was planted nearly everywhere for its intriguing ugliness. In some ways, it is as wild and ungainly as the young ginkgo trees planted everywhere along the streets of Washington, D.C.

Explanations for how the monkey puzzles got their wonderful name abound. Some commentators claim that monkeys are perplexed by their prickly leaves (how is a tender-footed monkey supposed to climb a prickly tree?). Others say that monkeys can climb up the trees but, because of their inextricable branches, can't figure out a way down. Still others insist that monkeys can't figure out how to climb *up* the trees. Perhaps the safest explanation is that monkeys have a devil of a time climbing both these trees because of their crazy branches and prickly leaves.

Care for monkey-puzzle trees is the same as for the Norfolk Island pine. Give them filtered or indirect light, preferably at a north window. Avoid direct sunlight except in winter. Provide cool temperatures on fall and winter nights between 55 and 65 degrees. Always allow the top of the soil to become powder-dry between thorough waterings. Avoid soggy soil and always empty the drainage dish. Fertilize as often as every two months, or as seldom as once a year for slower growth. Trees prefer to be pot-bound and only need repotting every four or five years. Slow-growing, they reach about one hundred feet outdoors, but they may take ten or even twenty years to reach your ceiling.

Monkey-puzzle tree (*Araucaria bidwillii*).

Norfolk Island Pine
(Araucaria excelsa)

The Norfolk Island pine has a reputation for being a hardy tree indoors, and it is often praised for its resemblance to the Christmas tree. But the tree seems to behave more hardily for some people than for others. One woman we know grew a Norfolk Island pine for twenty years. Other friends have had theirs die within a week, six months, or a year. The tree is one of the most beautiful on earth, but don't be too surprised if it gives you some trouble.

The Norfolk Island pine that lived for twenty years is a nice exception to our warning, so let it serve as an example of at least one way to grow the tree indoors.

The woman bought her tree in 1954 when it was three feet tall. By 1975 it had grown to seven feet. *In all those years, the only thing she ever did to it was water it once a week.* She never fertilized it, never changed its soil, never moved it to a larger pot. For twenty years, she swears she never did a thing to it but water it. The tree stood by a north window behind a partially open blind. In the winter the room was fairly cool, around 65 degrees.

We do not suggest that you grow your Norfolk Island pine exactly the way this woman grew hers. As a general rule, the tree should be fertilized at least once a year and repotted every four or five years. Because the woman did not do these things, her tree grew very slowly and did not need a larger pot. But she did do several things exactly right.

For one thing, she kept the tree in a cool room in the winter. Cool air is just what the Norfolk Island pine needs. It did much better indoors in the nineteenth century before the invention of central heating. Today, any number of Norfolk Island pines are perishing because the heat inside is too high and the air too dry. If it is at all possible, try to keep the tree in a room where the temperature drops to 65 degrees or lower on winter nights. The ideal night temperature is about 55 degrees, although the tree tolerates temperatures as low as 40 degrees. Norfolk Island is a tiny piece of land located about five hundred miles due east of Australia in the subtropical zone. This means that the tree is used to getting some cool air during part of the year.

The woman also gave her tree exactly the kind of lighting it needs. Too much hot direct sunlight will dry its needles out like an old Christmas tree. But filtered light coming through a partially open blind at a north window is ideal. In the winter, it will stand direct sunlight, but not at any other time of year.

The woman also watered her tree once a week, which is an excellent schedule for a Norfolk Island pine in a fairly small pot. If the pot had been ten inches or larger, she might have waited a bit longer and watered it every eight or ten days. The tree should be watered thoroughly and then not watered again until the top of the soil is powder-dry. Never let the root ball become soggy, but also never let it dry out.

We suspect that one of the main reasons the woman's tree lived so long is that

Norfolk Island pine (*Araucaria excelsa*).

she never moved it. It adapted to one place in her house and lived there happily for twenty years. Several plant shop owners have told us that they think the tree is sensitive to being touched and moved around.

As a matter of fact, the second the woman moved her tree, it died. She and her husband moved to a new house last year, and the tree picked up a lethal case of spider mites. It died within three weeks.

If the foregoing makes it sound as if the Norfolk Island pine is a delicate tree, in many cases it is. It may live for decades with proper care, but it could just as easily die tomorrow if you give it too much sunlight, too much water, and too stuffy a room. It is a pine tree, after all, even though it does come from a semi-tropical island, and pine trees have a tendency to dry out indoors. Try to think of it as a tree that likes nothing better than fresh, misty air. Misting its leaves daily in winter helps.

The Norfolk Island pine doesn't grow very fast—three to six inches a year—and some years it may not grow at all. It may not grow for several years, and then one spring it will surprise you and grow a bright new leader at the top. You can feed it as seldom as once a year, or as often as once every two months, but cut the recommended dosage in half. Either way, the tree won't grow much faster. For this reason, you will only need to repot it every four or five years. Use ordinary commercial potting soil.

Commercial growers propagate the tree by clipping off the leader and planting the side shoots in moist sand. However, this method will spoil the appearance of your tree and should not be attempted unless the tree has grown too large.

The tree appreciates a daily misting in the winter, which will brighten up its needles and help discourage pests. If you notice any insects on your tree, the best way to kill them is to place a Shell No-Pest Strip in a plastic bag and cover the tree for twenty-four hours. The needles of the Norfolk Island pine are so delicate that a stronger insecticide might do them permanent harm. You can help prevent a bug attack by hanging a No-Pest Strip in the same room as the tree. In fact, this is a good way to protect all your indoor plants and trees.

Palms

Palms have been used for centuries as decorative indoor trees. Their popularity reached its peak in Victorian days, when they flourished in hotel lobbies, restaurants, conservatories, and all those dark, oak-paneled sitting rooms, where they were just about the only plants that would survive.

There are over twelve thousand species of palms in the huge Palmaceae family, growing all over the world in all different shapes and sizes. Most of them prefer the tropics, but some species are subtropical and even temperate. It is strange to realize, for instance, that palms are planted in the streets of Dublin.

All palms share several peculiar characteristics. Their trunks do not have any interior growth rings or real branches and the life force or heart of the trees resides in a cabbage-like bud at the top of the trunk. The bud happens to taste good and is extremely vulnerable to animals such as monkeys—or, for that matter, men—and to high winds and disease. You can see dead palms along the beaches of Florida which look as stark as telephone poles. Many of them died because of damage to their buds. Their long, glorious fronds fell off until only the bare column of their trunks remained. Luckily, evolution took care to provide many species of palms with spiky trunks or spiny fronds in order to protect the vital bud from attack. It is interesting, though, that on certain islands and in certain regions where threatening animals did not live, the trees never bothered to develop this protective armor.

Palms are fascinating and incredibly versatile trees. Aside from decoration in homes, they serve as an important source of lumber, fruit, sugar, wine, starch, wax, fiber, oil, resin, and drugs. Economically speaking, they are among the most valuable and essential trees in the world. Considering the enormous number of species of palms on earth, it is not surprising that some palms make excellent indoor trees. Out of twelve thousand species, perhaps five or six are virtually indestructible indoors. Other species are sometimes used, but they are far more delicate and require greater care.

Most of the palms mentioned in the following essays are fairly easy to grow indoors. As a general rule, they abhor direct sunlight and need constantly moist, but not soggy, soil. The quickest way to damage an indoor palm is to expose it to direct sunlight in the spring. Most species will tolerate sunlight in the winter, but beginning in late February or early March, they should be moved into indirect or filtered light. Always keep the soil of a palm tree moist to the touch, but do not turn the soil into mud, and do not let the pot stand in water. Palms can just as easily die of drowning as of drought. The best method is to water them when just the top of the soil dries out. The trees grow well in ordinary commercial potting soil. However, keep them practically root-bound and only repot them every four or five years. Repotting interrupts their growth and invites the danger of *overpotting*, which in turn can lead to *overwatering* and rotting roots. Most palms can be fed once a month from early spring through summer with a water-soluble fertilizer, then feeding should be discontinued until the following spring. A timed-release fertilizer will provide more even feeding and may help to speed up growth.

But palms do not grow very fast. The best way to make one grow is to plant it in the garden in warm spring or summer in its pot. Do not expose it to direct sun. Keep the tree in full shade most of the day until late afternoon.

You cannot buy a one-foot palm and hope to see it grow into a tree overnight. Palms are nowhere near as lively as rubber trees, scheffleras, or dumb cane. They require patience, but they do grow. If you want size, buy a large palm to start with. If you want action—if you crave to see new growth—plant the pot outside.

Palms are great survivors. They add a beautiful tropical touch to any room. Our whole downstairs is painted white and accented with palms. We clip off yellowed or discolored leaves, along with browning tips, to keep them looking fresh and green. There is no way to avoid such blemishes, so do not be concerned if some leaves do this. Bugs have never been a problem. We dust the fronds and clean out cobwebs when we get a chance, but we do not mist the leaves. The foliage of most palms should be kept dry. One of our palms is still recuperating from a severe sunburn it received this spring, but otherwise we have found palms fairly easy to grow (although their fronds are rarely as green as we would like them to be). One or two of the following species may give you trouble, but the rest should live for years.

Areca palm (*Chrysalidocarpus lutescens*)—Second only to the kentia palm in

Areca palm (*Chrysalidocarpus lutescens*).

hardiness, and far more available, the areca palm is easily identified by its clusters of thin, yellow-green stalks and graceful, feathery fronds. Sold both as a small pot plant and as a five- or 6-foot clump (we hesitate to call it a tree), the areca does best in bright light but not direct sunlight. Do not put it in direct sunlight except in winter. Keep its soil evenly moist but not wet, allowing just the top of the soil to become dry between thorough waterings. Do not let it sit in water, and resist the temptation to water it every day. Fertilize it once a month from April through October, then discontinue feeding until the following spring. From Madagascar, this palm is one of the most reliable indoor plants you can buy. Some people claim the areca will grow as much as ten inches a year, although ours has never even come close to attaining that rate of growth. Be sure to keep your areca in the shade if you put it outside.

Bamboo palm (*Chamaedorea erumpens*)—This palm is an excellent substitute for real bamboo. It grows like bamboo from thin, cane-like stalks, but it is much hardier than bamboo indoors. Its leaves are slightly broader and less delicate than real bamboo. From Honduras, it is an ideal indoor tree since it actually prefers shade over bright light or direct sun. Bright light will dry it out, and direct sun will burn its leaves. Keep the soil moist at all times but not soaking wet. Allow the top of the soil to become powder-dry between drenchings with tepid water. Fertilize once a month from early spring through early fall, then discontinue feeding until the following spring. It likes house temperatures and does not need cool winter nights. Never expose it to frost. The plant will grow to eight feet, but it will take a small one many years to attain that size indoors.

Chinese fan palm (*Livistona chinensis*)—The fan-shaped leaves on this exotic Chinese palm are large and can stretch almost two feet across. The lower half of the leaves are pleated like open fans, while the upper halves are split into segments

Chinese fan palm (*Livistona chinensis*). (Photo by McDonald/Mulligan)

like broad fingers or claws. The leaf stems are covered with sharp spines. While the description may sound ferocious, the Chinese fan palm is extremely attractive and fairly easy to grow indoors. It is not as widely available as some palms, but if you like to collect palms and have the space, this one is intriguing and worth the price. Give the tree bright indirect light or curtain-filtered light, but avoid direct sun. Keep the soil evenly moist at all times, allowing the surface to become dry between waterings. Do not water it every day. Fertilize once a month through spring and summer, but let the plant rest in fall and winter. It prefers cool air in the sixties at night during the winter, but never expose it to frost. Most Chinese fan palms are sold with a short, rough trunk no more than one to two feet tall. The plant is very broad but not particularly tall.

European fan palm (*Chamaerops humilis*)—This is one of the few indoor palms that prefers direct sunlight. It will tolerate lower light, but it won't grow quite as actively. Like all palms, its soil needs to be kept constantly moist. Water it thoroughly when just the surface of the soil becomes powder-dry. Resist the impulse to pamper it and kill it with too much water, but don't turn your back on it, either, for more than a week. From the Mediterranean regions of southern Europe and northern Africa, the plant is low and bushy like the Chinese fan palm, but different in the structure of its stems and leaves. The stems are spineless and rise from rough trunks covered with a black, hairy fiber. While fan-shaped, the leaves are far more segmented and stiffer, like spikes, and they do not meld together into a solid leaf at the base. This species is just as hardy, if not slightly hardier, than its counterpart from China.

European fan palm (*Chamaerops humilis*). (Photo by T. H. Everett)

Fishtail palm (*Caryota mitis*).

Fishtail palm (*Caryota mitis*)—The corrugated, triangular leaves of this palm look very much like fishtails. It is as if a hundred or a thousand fishtails were hanging from one tree. From Burma, Malaya, and Indonesia, the tree is extremely hardy indoors if kept in bright indirect light or bright curtain-filtered light. It will look spindly grown in shade, and its leaves will burn in direct sun. Keep its soil wet at all times (it should feel moist when you press it with your finger), but do not let it get soggy. Fertilize it once a month from early spring through summer, then do not feed it until the following spring. The tree prefers warm temperatures and likes dry air. It can grow to twenty-five feet, but the normal size available in stores is one to five feet. The fishtail palm is unusual and different-looking, a good conversation piece, but its leaves are often ragged at the edges, as if they had been chewed on by a larger fish. Be selective and wait until you find a handsome specimen.

Kentia palm (*Howea forsteriana*)—Long recognized as the most hardy of all the indoor palms, the kentia has large, dark green, leathery leaves on soaring stems. From Lord Howe Island off the coast of Australia, it can grow to sixty feet outdoors. A specimen nearly that size recently toppled over at the U. S. Botanic Gardens in Washington, D.C. Its tremendous, spreading crown had simply grown too heavy for its slender trunk. Without notice, without even a breath of wind, it just snapped and crashed to the ground one summer night. The next day, when employees came to work, they found the palm house infinitely brighter than they had in years. Although the kentia won't grow to sixty feet in your living room, it may live long enough to force you out of your house. It grows best in bright indirect light or behind a thin light curtain in a brightly lighted place. Keep the soil moist at all times, but not soggy or really soaking wet. When you press your finger to the soil, it should always feel moist. Feed the tree once a month through spring and summer, then discontinue feeding until the following spring. The kentia prefers cool night temperatures in the sixties in the winter. The only trouble with this beautiful tree is that it is not that easy to find.

Lady palm (*Rhapis excelsa*)—From southern China, the lady palm is unusual-looking with its thin, rectangular leaves which fan out from slender stalks like fingers on a hand. Its feminine name is appropriate for small plants where only the delicate leaves show. But taller specimens have stems covered with a dark, hairy fiber and could just as easily be called "hirsute palms" or "male palms." The tree is sometimes available in sizes up to six feet. Give the lady palm bright filtered light, the brighter the better, but not direct sun. Keep its soil evenly moist at all times but not soggy. Fertilize it once a month through spring and summer.

Lady palm (*Rhapis excelsa*). (Photo by Terrestris, N.Y.C.)

Parlor palm (*Chamaedorea elegans*). (Photo by McDonald/Mulligan)

Parlor palm (*Chamaedorea elegans,* also called *Neanthe bella*)—One of the mainstays of the old Victorian sitting room, this dwarf species of palm has classic, feathery fronds and green stems ringed with white. It is extremely hardy and practically impossible to kill, but its foliage tends to discolor and burn, and often the plant looks dry. It prefers moderate shade to bright light, which makes it ideal for locations where other houseplants won't survive. Direct sunlight in spring and summer will almost immediately burn its leaves. Give the plant moist soil at all times. Water it as soon as the top of the soil becomes dry, but don't kill it with love by hovering over it and watering it every day. Its roots need oxygen, and too much water will simply drown the plant. From Mexico, this charming and manageable plant rarely grows above three feet.

Pygmy date palm (*Phoenix roebelenii*)—The pygmy date palm is one of the few indoor palms that really has a trunk. One of our personal favorites, it is sold as a two-to-four-foot tree with rough brown bark and delicate, arching, symmetrical fronds. Its great appeal to us is that it looks almost exactly like a tall, mature, tropical palm—except that it is small and can fit in your house. Most of the other indoor palms are little more than tall plants with thin stems. We heartily recommend this tree if you can afford it and have the space. It needs bright light and moist soil and will really appreciate spending the summer outdoors. Grown in a tub, it looks perfect standing out on the front steps. Water the tree thoroughly, then allow the very top of the soil to become powder-dry before watering it thoroughly again. Indoors it will need bright curtain-filtered light or bright indirect light against a light wall. Fertilize an established tree once a month through spring and summer, but do not feed it during the winter months. The tree likes dry air, so do not mist its fronds. The pygmy date is not quite as hardy as some indoor palms, but it should live a long time if you treat it well. From Laos and Vietnam, it can grow to seven or eight feet, but it grows very slowly indoors.

Pygmy date palm (*Phoenix roebelenii*).

Pencil Cactus
(Euphorbia tirucallii)

Few trees on earth are stranger-looking than this extremely hardy succulent from Zanzibar, Uganda, and the Congo. Some people like its looks and others don't, but there is no disputing the fact that it is virtually indestructible indoors. If you give the tree bright light and keep its soil barely moist all year, it should be one of the longest-lived of all your indoor plants and trees.

Available nearly everywhere, and often in sizes up to five or six feet, the pencil cactus is not a true cactus but a succulent belonging to the same family as the poinsettia. It is so tough that it grows on sand dunes in Florida and helps to keep them from blowing away. [A stem cutting from a pencil cactus can grow as much as eight feet in one year.] The tree will reach your ceiling in two or three years if you do not prune it. There is a tall pencil cactus growing at the U. S. Botanic Gardens in Washington, D.C. It has a smooth, symmetrical, perfectly ordinary trunk, topped by an unbelievable tangle of green hair. The tree can grow to thirty feet and has a poisonous, milky sap which can make a person ill if he chews on a branch. While you may never chew on one, a child conceivably might.

Pencil cactus (*Euphorbia tirucallii*).

What makes the pencil cactus so unique is that its branches seem to have no leaves. Small leaves do grow on it, but they fall off almost as soon as they appear. From a distance, the tree looks stark and dead, like a hairy tumbleweed. But up close its branches are light green and very much alive. The branches are smooth, cylindrical, and about the thickness of a pencil, and thus the origin of its common name.

The pencil cactus will live forever if you water it properly, but it will rot and die if you don't. Do not pamper it with constant watering. Its succulent branches hold water longer than you might think. Always allow the top two inches of the soil to become powder-dry. Resist the urge to water it every day or every other day or even every week. Wait until it's dry. Then drench it and allow it to dry out again. Never let the container stand in water. In winter, when it is resting, water it even less.

The tree will grow best in bright direct sunlight at a south window, but it will do almost as well in bright filtered light or indirect light against a light wall. Avoid constant shade. If natural light is unavailable, give it strong artificial light with a 150-watt bulb for at least twelve hours a day.

Fertilize the pencil cactus only once a year in spring, and do not fertilize a newly purchased tree at all for the first year.

Repot at any season when the roots begin to overcrowd the pot. Use a mixture of half potting soil and half sharp sand.

Perhaps because of its poisonous sap, or because it has so few leaves, the tree is almost never bothered by insects.

Night temperatures of 55 to 65 degrees are what the pencil cactus likes best in winter, but it won't complain if you prefer a warmer house.

To propagate the pencil cactus, cut off several branches with a pair of scissors or a knife and wash off the sap from the base of each clipping. Store the clippings in a cool, shady place for several days or a week. After they have dried, plant them in barely moist sand or in potting soil. Do not sink them deep into the soil or they may rot. If you grow the clippings outside in spring or summer, they will shoot up faster into a large, but forever strange, tree.

Pleomele reflexa

You will have to do some searching to find a tall *Pleomele reflexa* such as the seven-foot specimen in the picture. And if you find one, the price may be prohibitive. The scarceness and cost of a tall reflexa is unfortunate, since we think the plant looks infinitely better as a tree than as a two-or-three-foot pot plant, which is the way it is usually sold.

There are a number of different species of pleomeles available, among them the *P. reflexa variegata,* the *P. thalioides,* and the *P. augustifolia variegata.* As pot plants, all three species are normally better-looking than the reflexa. But the advantage of the reflexa is that it makes a hardy and striking indoor tree.

The reflexa is distinguished by dark green, shiny, lance-shaped leaves, six to

Pleomele reflexa.

eight inches long, which are set unusually close together on slender stems. The trouble with a small reflexa is that its leaves are so abundant that the stems really can't support the weight of all the leaves. The result is often a plant with comically bent and twisting stems. A small reflexa looks like those frilly toothpicks used to decorate hams—except that the toothpicks happen to be warped.

The main point in the reflexa's favor, especially when it reaches tree size, is that it belongs to the liliaceae family, which includes such hardy indoor species as the dracaenas and the yuccas. In other words, the reflexa is very tough. It tolerates low light and likes soil on the dry side.

For the reflexa to look its best, water it liberally and then allow the top one to two inches of the soil to become powder-dry before watering it again.

While the tree will tolerate low light, it will actively grow in high diffuse light, such as behind a thin light curtain, or in bright indirect light against a light wall. It will also grow in any window with an exposure other than a southern one. Direct light from the south may scorch its leaves and dry the plant out. The tree thrives in high humidity. To increase moisture in the air around it in the winter, place it close to other foliage plants or set the pot in a pan filled with pebbles and water. Fertilize it every three months year-round.

The variegated reflexa, *P. reflexa variegata,* has lush green leaves with beautiful yellow edges. The plant requires high light and is more suited to the greenhouse than the home. Like the simple reflexa, it can grow up to twelve feet, but it grows slowly and will take forever to become a tree if you buy it small.

Native to India and islands in the Indian Ocean, both species can be propagated by stem cuttings. They both like average temperatures, no lower than 55 degrees at night.

Poinsettia
(Euphorbia pulcherrima)

New varieties of this ever popular Christmas plant now make it possible to grow a poinsettia indoors without nearly as much trouble as in the past. The result is that many people now have small poinsettia trees growing in their homes year-round. The new varieties are less susceptible to drafts and do not need to be locked away in the basement or the garage before and after Christmas. They hold their color longer, too. They grow fast and will begin to look like trees in less than a year if you do not cut them back. Even the most recent books on indoor gardening still give complicated instructions for growing them, but thanks to the new varieties, much of what they say can now be overlooked. (There is little need to worry about getting saddled with an old variety of poinsettia, since all the growers now prefer the new ones.)

The poinsettia is famous for clusters of brilliant red leaves, called bracts, which appear on the plant in a burst of glory in late fall. The bracts serve the purpose of

White poinsettia (*Euphorbia pulcherrima alba cv.*). (Photo by Genereux Library)

attracting bees to the inconspicuous yellow flowers which appear in the center of the leaves. Other varieties of poinsettia grow pink, yellow, or white bracts. The plant is Mexican in origin and grows to twelve feet high or more outdoors. It was introduced to the United States early in the nineteenth century by J. R. Poinsett, who was U. S. Minister to Mexico.

Poinsettias need bright light or direct sunlight and soil on the dry side to grow well indoors. They resent drafts and will drop leaves in a location where temperatures fluctuate, but at least the new varieties are more tolerant to cold than their predecessors. Keep them near a warm, bright window and always allow the surface of the soil to become powder-dry between thorough waterings. Resist the urge to water every day or every other day. Be patient and wait until the top of the soil dries out. Then empty the dish in which the pot stands.

If you buy or receive a poinsettia at Christmas, it may retain its color until Easter or even as late as June. Then it will gradually drop its colored leaves and begin to grow new green ones at the same time. The taller it gets, the less spectacular it will look each succeeding winter, since the majority of its leaves will still be green, even if red bracts do appear in late fall. Moreover, the new bracts will only turn red, pink, yellow, or white *if you put the plant in a location where it receives the same rhythm of daylight and nighttime as the vegetation outside.* All this means is that the plant should not be exposed to electric light in your home once night falls. Beginning in October, put it by a bright window in a room that you do not use at night. You don't have to move it to a closet every night, unless your home does not have a spare back room. The plant is ideal in a sunny office window where the lights go off every night promptly at six.

If you love the poinsettia for its color and don't care much for its green leaves, prune it radically in August down to about eight inches. This will stimulate more vigorous and numerous growth of the bracts in late fall. However, pruning it will prevent the plant from ever attaining tree size. If you want a tree, let it grow tall for a year or two before you start to prune.

The poinsettia requires a rather odd feeding schedule to look its best. During its flowering period from September through mid-December feed it every ten days with a water-soluble fertilizer diluted to half the recommended strength. Do not feed it at all from mid-December through February. Beginning in March, feed it once a month until September.

The plant will grow rapidly if you put it outside when the weather warms up and keep it out all summer. The best method is to plunge it in the garden in its pot. It should put on a foot of new growth by fall if treated this way.

Poinsettias can be propagated with great ease from cuttings in the summer or early fall. Plant the cuttings in moist potting soil and cover the pot with plastic wrap. New roots will set in about three weeks. Keep the cuttings out of direct sunlight for the first several weeks. When you initially take the cuttings, be sure to plant them before the leaves wilt, or keep them in water until you have the time to pot them.

As a poinsettia grows taller, it will develop a rather skinny stem or stems with foliage growing near the top. To be blunt it will get leggy. However, the effect is interesting and not always unattractive.

Wait about two years before repotting a poinsettia you have just received. Use ordinary commercial potting soil when repotting.

Ponytail Palm

(Beaucarnea recurvata) also called elephant-foot tree

This tree is practically impossible to kill. It will live forever if you water it correctly and keep it in bright light. Never water it until the top of the soil is powder-dry (and even then, hold off watering a few days longer until it is *really* dry). The odd and amazing trunk of the ponytail palm is like a camel's hump. It is built for desert life to hold water and withstand drought. The price of overwatering is death. On the other hand, the great advantage of this tree indoors is that it can take care of itself when you go away on trips. We've let ours go for as long as a month without watering it.

From Mexico, the ponytail is not a true palm tree but a member of the Liliaceae or lily family. It is related to the corn plant and the yucca tree, both of which are very tough. Above its swollen trunk grows a cluster of long, thin, downward-curving, grassy-green leaves. The effect is somewhat like a gushing fountain—or a ponytail. The thick trunk is reminiscent of an elephant's foot, thus its other common name.

The tree is widely available in sizes from one to three feet, and can occasionally be found as an eight-foot monster with a trunk four feet across. Slow-growing, outdoors it can eventually reach a height of thirty feet with a trunk fifteen feet thick or

Ponytail palm (*Beaucarnea recurvata*).

more. We once saw an ancient ponytail palm growing on the grounds of an estate near Orlando, Florida. An executive at nearby Walt Disney World was interested in buying it for the park, but when a tree expert came to look at it, he shook his head and said the tree would cost a fortune to move. It must have weighed twenty or thirty tons.

Give the ponytail palm direct sunlight at any exposure or, failing the presence of direct light, keep it in the brightest spot in your home. It will need strong artificial lighting with a 150-watt bulb kept three feet above the leaves for twelve hours a day if natural light is unavailable.

Always drench the soil thoroughly with tepid water. Make sure all the soil gets moist, then empty the drainage dish of excess water. Leave the tree alone for many days or even weeks until the top of the soil is powder-dry. If you have a large tree in a container twelve inches in diameter or more, wait until the top of the soil is dry two inches down. For smaller pots, be sure you can pick up enough dry soil to sift through your hands.

The ponytail can go for years without repotting, so resist the impulse to repot it every year. When you do repot it every five or six years, use ordinary commercial potting soil mixed with an equal amount of rough sand. Increase the size of the pot by no more than a few inches, since the tree does best when nearly root-bound.

Do not feed the tree at all for the first year. Then only feed it once a year, preferably in early spring. The tree is so slow-growing that it can't absorb excess amounts of food. Do not expect it to grow more than a foot every five or ten years.

Privet
(Ligustrum lucidum)

Privet is one of the most attractive and popular hedge plants in America, but in recent years it has also begun to appear in tropical plant stores as a pot-grown indoor tree. Some species grow to thirty feet outdoors, and they are easily identified by their beautiful, shiny, dark green, one-to-two-inch leaves and pale gray, woody stems.

The plant belongs to the olive family and is related to such sweet-smelling shrubs as the lilac, jasmine, and forsythia.

Privet is one of the easiest indoor trees to prune and shape, but it needs very bright light, cool night air, and a minimum of watering in winter to survive indoors. Keeping it alive in winter is definitely a challenge. The tree is worth considering if you can provide it with a bright but cool location, but avoid it if you live in a dimly lit apartment where you can't control the heat.

Although privet grows like a weed from California south to Texas and as far north as New England, it is actually native to Japan, China, and Korea, where it is often used in the art of bonsai. Even as a bonsai tree, it is not normally kept indoors for more than a short period of time. When you realize that the plant can survive winter snows and freezing temperatures, you may begin to question its adaptability as an indoor tree.

Privet (*Ligustrum lucidum*). (Photo by T. H. Everett)

The major problem with a privet grown indoors in winter is that it will defoliate almost completely unless you give it proper care. The first thing to do is to reduce the watering drastically so it can rest. Only water it two or three times from December through February. Drench the whole pot, but then let it become dry. On the other hand, mist the foliage daily if you can. This will discourage leaf drop. A small privet will benefit from being placed in a tray filled with pebbles and water, but this method of increasing humidity won't work for a specimen three or four feet tall. If you own a humidifier, keep it going in the same room as the plant.

Give your privet direct sunlight in all seasons, preferably in a window facing south. If it is not getting enough light, place it under a strong light bulb for five or six hours every night.

Cool air in winter is of major importance. A sun porch where the temperature does not drop below freezing or a drafty entranceway are both excellent locations for the tree. Keep the privet as far away from heating units or a lighted fireplace as possible. Night temperatures of 40 to 55 degrees are ideal. The energy crisis should be a boon for this tree, especially in homes where hardy people set their thermostats down to 50 degrees.

The last thing to remember is: never fertilize this tree in winter; discontinue feeding as early as September 1.

While these requirements may sound complicated, they all boil down to bright light, cool air, little water, high humidity, and no food. If your privet is suffering during the winter it is probably from too little or too much of any one or all five of these things.

In spring, summer, and early fall, water the privet when the top of the soil becomes thoroughly dry. It is not a heavy water drinker. If the plant is in a pot twelve inches in diameter or more, wait until the top of the soil is dry one to two inches down. Resist the urge to water every day or every other day, but give the soil a good drenching when the surface dries out. Then always empty the drainage dish in which the pot stands.

Privet also needs direct sunlight or very bright indirect light during the warm months. We strongly advise putting the plant outside in spring and summer to revive it after the winter indoors. It will grow fast and beautifully out on the front steps or plunged into the garden in its pot. But bring it back inside before winter, since its roots will freeze unless the pot is kept underground and protected with mulch.

Feed the tree once every two months from April to August with a water-soluble plant food, or use a timed-release fertilizer following the instructions on the label.

Privet is especially easy to propagate by planting cuttings in moist potting soil and covering them with plastic wrap. The best time to do this is in spring or summer. The more cuttings you start, the greater your chances of success. If you have privet growing in your yard, take some cuttings and try growing them indoors.

Dry air around the tree in winter will invite an infestation of spider mites, so be sure to mist the leaves and keep them clean. Use Isotox or Systemic on these pests if they appear and won't wash off.

Privet reacts better to pruning than almost any other indoor tree. You can clip away the lower branches to accentuate the trunk and thin out the leaves to reveal the inner structure of the tree. The best time to prune it is in spring or early summer and then again in the fall.

Sago Palm

(Cycas revoluta) also called pineapple palm

From one of the most primitive plant families on earth (Cycadaceae), the sago palm is a tough, slow-growing, extremely attractive palm-like tree with hard, sharp, highly polished dark green fronds one to seven feet long. It first appeared on earth over 200 million years ago. Although it looks like a palm tree, it is not. It also bears no relation to the true sago palms, which produce a white powdery starch called sago.

From south Japan and Java, the sago eventually grows a trunk six to ten feet tall, but specimens that size are extremely old and virtually unheard of in plant stores. The tree is normally sold with fronds one to four feet long growing out of a thick, brown, bulbous base that resembles a pineapple or a pine cone. We have sometimes heard the tree called pineapple palm.

Even a small sago with fronds only a foot long can be expensive ($15 and up) in a northern plant store, although we bought a beautiful plant that size in Florida for under $5. The only trouble with the sago is that its leathery foliage damages easily when knocked around. If damage is severe, you can cut off all the fronds

Sago palm (*Cycas revoluta*).

and start from scratch. The plant will eventually grow new fronds, but only over the course of several years.

The sago is fairly hardy indoors and requires little care. It looks superb and is ideal for tropical effect. But don't expect it to perform like a schefflera or a rubber tree; the plant is just plain slow. It may produce one or two new fronds every year, or it may not. Whatever you do, don't sit around waiting for it to grow. It will drive you crazy. The best thing to do is turn your back on it and let the appearance of a new frond come as a surprise. When new growth finally does appear, it will arrive in the form of a long, skinny shoot like a new frond on a fern. The shoot will have small ringlets on it which will gradually uncoil like a bishop's crosier and finally straighten out into individual leaves. Florida growers differentiate between the 'King' sago, which has hard, sharp, pointed leaves, and the 'Queen' sago, whose leaves look similar but feel softer and more pliable. The King sago seems to be the more prevalent of the two varieties on the northern market at the present time.

The sago needs a very well-lighted position. Keep it in sunlight in fall and winter, then move it into bright diffuse light in spring and summer. It will discolor and do poorly in low light. Give it sixteen hours of artificial illumination with a 150-watt grow light if natural light is unavailable.

The tree should be drenched and then allowed to become moderately dry. Always wait until the top one to two inches of the soil are powder-dry before soaking the soil with tepid water. Then empty the drainage dish of excess water.

The sago will do best with cool night temperatures in winter between 50 and 65 degrees, but it will tolerate warmer night air.

Do not mist its fronds. It likes dry air.

Feed the tree every two months from early spring through summer, then discontinue feeding until the following spring. Do not fertilize it for the first six months at least.

The sago can be propagated with suckers growing from its base.

When roots begin to overcrowd the pot, transfer the sago in spring to a container two inches larger using fresh, all-purpose potting soil.

Another palm-like cycad which we have occasionally seen is the amazing *Zamia furfuracea* or "cardboard palm." The tree has perhaps the stiffest, hardest, most unreal-feeling leaves of all the indoor trees. The leaves are elliptical, two to four inches long, waxy green on top, and covered with fuzz beneath. The name *furfuracea* means "scurfy" in Greek and is wonderfully appropriate for this tree. The cardboard palm grows a trunk four to five feet tall and needs direct sunlight and soil kept on the moist side. Water it when just the surface of the soil dries out. From Mexico and Colombia, it is an intriguing tree, but not particularly warm or comfortable because of its incredibly hard leaves.

Schefflera or Umbrella Tree

(Brassaia actinophylla)

This hardy and fast-growing Australian tree is a *must* if you have visions of trying to turn an ordinary houseplant into a tree. Expect it to grow a foot or more a year with proper care. It reaches over thirty feet outdoors, and specimens of ten or fifteen feet are now a common sight in office buildings and shopping malls. While it has been popular as a houseplant for some time, the schefflera is often available in plant shops now as a five-or-six-foot tree.

The schefflera derives its common name, umbrella tree, from its umbrella-like clusters of large, glossy, bright green leaves. When the plant is young, the clusters tend to grow from three to five leaves each. As the plant matures, the clusters increase their leaf production anywhere from eight leaves to a cluster up to sixteen. If you start with a plant bearing five leaves to a cluster and end up with a tree bearing eight leaves to a cluster or more, you've really achieved something.

A schefflera will suffer almost as much abuse as a rubber tree or a corn plant. The only thing it will not tolerate is incorrect watering.

When watering a schefflera, *always* allow the top of the soil to become powder-dry between thorough waterings. If the top of the soil is dark and still feels moist, don't water it. Do not think the tree will grow faster if you water it every day. On the contrary, its leaves will turn yellow and the tree will die. Feel the top of the soil with your fingers. Does it look gray and sift through your fingers like ash? If so, water it well enough so that water begins pouring out the drainage holes. Then

Schefflera (*Brassaia actinophylla*).

empty the drainage dish. Now forget the tree for five or six days. Even if a week or two weeks go by and the top of the soil is still moist, restrain yourself. Always follow the simple rule of waiting until the top of the soil is powder-dry. It may hurt at first, but you'll be thankful later on when you see how well the tree grows.

The schefflera will survive in fairly low light, which makes it useful in dim apartments where many houseplants won't survive. But it really prefers bright light or even direct sunlight. We have two very large scheffleras which we bought as one-foot pot plants three years ago. They have grown a foot a year sitting in the bay window in our living room, which faces northeast. Even when we have exposed them to full sun in spring and summer, their leaves haven't burned. On the other hand, we have another schefflera which we bought at the same time but kept in low light upstairs. Today the plant is only half the size of our two big "scheffs" downstairs.

If you are really ambitious to grow a schefflera fast, the best thing to do is keep it outside in warm weather. But put it under a covered porch or heavy shade tree for two weeks to acclimatize it to outdoor light. Hose the leaves down often to keep them clean and free of pests. Insects will naturally be more drawn to the plant outdoors.

Since the tree grows fast under ideal conditions, you may have to repot it every year or every other year. Use ordinary commercial potting soil when repotting and step up the size of the container by one or two inches.

The tree can be fed as often as once a month in spring and summer if you use a water-soluble fertilizer. For rapid growth, your best bet is a timed-release fertilizer. For slower growth, only feed the plant two or three times a year.

The schefflera can be propagated by rooting a new leaf shoot in a glass of water. When the shoot develops roots, plant it in a small pot filled with commercial potting soil. You might also find it intriguing to grow a schefflera from seed. The only company we know which carries schefflera seeds is Park Seed Co., Inc., Greenwood, S.C. 29647. Don't expect immediate shipment and don't expect all the seeds to grow. Tropical plant seeds tend to dry out rapidly, which is why so few seed companies carry them.

The most common troubles to expect from scheffleras are yellowing of the leaves, which usually indicates too much watering (unless, of course, you've forgotten to water the tree for over a month, in which case the leaves are yellow because the tree is too dry), and black or brown spots on the leaves. The spots are a sign of a fungus called alternaria, and the best thing to do is remove the damaged leaves. If the fungus threatens to destroy the entire plant, resort to using either Zineb or Captan.

The schefflera comes close to being our favorite indoor tree. We heartily recommend it to you.

Screw Pine

(Pandanus utilis)

Here is a striking foliage plant with long, beautiful, shiny green leaves and sawtoothed edges colored either white or dark red. Some species, such as *P. utilis* from Madagascar, grow thirty to sixty feet outdoors, but indoor specimens do not usually have a trunk. Indoors, they resemble an overgrown pineapple plant, but their leaves are shinier and much more graceful-looking. The screw pine can grow huge in your home, with leaves as long as three feet. It is an excellent choice if you are just beginning to grow trees indoors. It will survive in shade as well as in bright light and will forgive you if you forget to water it. But put the plant in an area where people will not brush against it, since its edges are devilishly sharp and may scratch you or rip your clothes. Otherwise, it has no disadvantages to speak of.

The screw pine is not a true pine tree, but it does produce cone-like fruit outdoors, which is where it gets the latter part of its common name. The first part comes from the fact that its leaves rise in a twisting, spiraling shape like the threads of a screw. The white-margined species, *P. veitchii* from Polynesia, is the hardiest species of screw pine, but the red-margined *P. utilis* grows almost as well indoors. Another species is the blue screw pine, *P. baptistii,* with blue-green leaves and a yellow center stripe, but it is harder to grow indoors and really requires a greenhouse to look its best.

The tree likes to have its soil drenched and then dried out. Never water it until the top one to two inches of the soil are powder-dry. Its leathery leaves hold moisture longer than many houseplants. If you water it every day or every other day, you will kill it. Have faith and be patient. When the top of the soil dries out, water

Screw pine (*Pandanus utilis*).

the pot well so that all the soil gets moist. Then empty the drainage dish in which the pot stands.

Lighting is no problem with this tree, since it survives in dim corners but also grows in bright, curtain-filtered light or indirect light. For rapid growth, keep it in a bright location, but do not expose it to scorching summer sun. It will grow best in the summer outdoors, but, again, avoid exposing it to direct sunlight. The tree is not especially fast-growing, so expect several years to pass before you notice a real increase in size.

Feed the screw pine only three or four times a year from early spring through fall, and do not fertilize it in the winter. Overfeeding will produce softer leaves that will turn yellow and spongy in bright light.

The tree likes a fairly small pot and will need repotting only every five or six years with commercial potting soil.

The screw pine can be propagated by transplanting the small offshoots which grow from its base. Remove these carefully with a knife and plant them in moist potting soil, vermiculite, or sand. Cover the pot with plastic wrap and keep it in a warm, bright place.

Over the course of time, the tree develops thick aerial roots for support. These can be left to hang over the sides of the pot or can be trained to grow into the soil. However, they are not essential to the life of the plant indoors and can be snipped off if you prefer.

Sea Grape

(Coccoloba uvifera)

This small tree does not grow very well indoors. It is often used in Florida as a landscape plant, but in recent years some people in the houseplant business have tried to pass it off as a hardy indoor tree. Since you may well run across a sea grape in a plant store, we urge you to think twice before you buy one. On the other hand, if you already have, read on.

Frankly, we like the sea grape or *Coccoloba uvifera* because of its name. Its looks are mediocre, but the gentle, gurgling, watery, almost bird-like sound of Coc-co-lo-ba is so rhythmical that it's almost lured us into buying the plant. The sea grape comes from the West Indies, but it also grows along the shores of southern Florida, and *Coccoloba* is not a West Indian name but Greek. It means "colored seed or fruit," while *uvifera* means "grape-bearing." The tree produces clusters of small round purple fruit that look like grapes. The fruit is edible and is sometimes made into preserves. But don't expect the tree to fruit indoors.

The sea grape grows to twenty feet outdoors and has round, shiny, pale green leaves five to eight inches across. The leaves have prominent red veins when

Sea grape (*Coccoloba uvifera*).

young, which turn an ivory color as they mature. Outdoors the foliage is striking, but indoors there is something just a little bit washed-out-looking about the yellowish cast to the leaves, and there aren't that many leaves growing on the slender, woody stem. The effect is rather sickly and bare.

When watering the sea grape, always allow the surface of the soil to become powder-dry. It is not a dry-soil plant compared to a cactus or a succulent, but it will still drown if you water it every day. Let the surface of the soil become ash-gray before you water it thoroughly with tepid water. When excess water has drained out the drainage holes, empty the dish in which the pot stands.

The tree needs full sunlight to survive indoors, or at the very least the brightest indirect light you can provide. A shadier location will cause it to produce smaller, darker leaves, and in time the tree will die.

Always keep the sea grape in a warm, draft-free place. It will not tolerate temperatures much below 60 degrees for long.

Feed the tree with a timed-release fertilizer, following the instructions on the package, for rapid growth. Or use a water-soluble plant food once a month in spring and summer. For slower growth, cut the feeding back to twice a year.

The tree will grow best in the spring, summer, and early fall if outdoors. Put it outside immediately in the spring if it has grown sickly during the winter indoors.

Propagation is by air layering (see page 50) or stem cutting.

There is a variegated variety of sea grape called *C. uvifera auria,* which is hard to find. There is also an enormous species called *C. grandifolia,* which is not commercially available and would look absurd indoors. The tree grows to eighty feet and has leaves four feet across! An amazing specimen is growing at the U. S. Botanic Gardens in Washington, D.C.

Silk Oak
(Grevillea robusta)

The silk oak rivals the avocado tree for rate of growth indoors. It is also one of the easiest indoor trees to grow from seed. A friend of ours has one that grew four feet from seed in the first year. The tree is easily identified by its lacy fern-like leaves growing from a thin willowy stem.

Native to Australia, the silk oak is no relation to the American or European oak. It belongs to the Proteaceae family, which includes over a thousand species of trees and shrubs, mainly from Australia, but also found in Asia, South America, and South Africa. It is sometimes planted as a street tree in California, where it grows to 150 feet. Its delicate leaves bear only a faint resemblance to the leaves of the common oak.

If you enjoy growing plants from seed, or are curious to try, the silk oak is a must. Growing trees from seed is inexpensive and fun, especially with a co-operative tree like the silk oak. To grow a silk oak from seed, simply place several seeds in a small pot filled with moist potting soil, cover them with a fine layer of soil no more than a half inch deep, and seal the top of the pot with plastic wrap. The

Silk oak (*Grevillea robusta*).

seeds should germinate in about two weeks. Keep the seedlings well watered in a bright place out of direct sunlight. When they are three or four inches tall, transplant them into individual pots. The best time to grow the seeds is in spring or summer.

Whether you buy a silk oak in a plant store or grow one from seed, you will need to give the plant bright light, cool air, and lots of water in the summer to make it thrive. A screened-in porch during warm weather is an ideal place to grow a silk oak for quick results. The leaves will let you know immediately when they need water, since they wilt. Feed it three or four times from early spring through fall with a water-soluble fertilizer. In the winter, keep it away from heating units near a bright cool window if you can.

The tree can also be propagated by making cuttings of new shoots in spring or summer and planting them in moist potting soil.

The silk oak looks its best at about a year and a half and then starts getting leggy. It will need to be propped up with a stake since its stem is so thin. For a time, you can hide the stem behind other plants or furniture, but eventually you may want to dispose of the tree. A smart idea is to have several silk oaks growing at once, starting the seeds at two or three month intervals.

The tree will do best in the winter with temperatures between 55 and 65 at night. Don't expose it to temperatures below 50 degrees for long.

Tree Ferns

Imagine a fern with a trunk one hundred feet tall and huge fronds fifteen feet long. Vast forests of such enormous tropical trees covered the earth long before the evolution of man. A few descendants of those amazing prehistoric tree ferns still exist in the jungles of Hawaii, Puerto Rico, Jamaica, Mexico, Australia, and New Zealand. All of them will do best in a greenhouse, but several species are now available as indoor trees.

If you have been successful with ferns in hanging baskets and small pots, you should not have too much trouble growing two species in particular: *Cibotium schiedei,* the Mexican tree fern, and *C. chamissoi,* from Hawaii. But several other species are much trickier to grow, and you should definitely ask for the name of the tree before you buy.

Watch out especially for *Alsophila cooperi,* the Australian tree fern, which usually requires a greenhouse to survive. *Cyathea arborea,* from Puerto Rico and Jamaica, is sold as an indoor tree, but it requires high humidity and may perish in a bone-dry, centrally heated home. The New Zealand tree fern, *Dicksonia squarrosa,* is also difficult and needs very cool night air.

Your best bet is to stick with either of the two cibotiums—and the hardier of

Mexican tree fern (*Cibotium schiedei*). (Photo T. H. Everett)

these trees is the Mexican tree fern, *C. schiedei,* which is really the only tree fern which can stand dry air.

Smaller plant stores rarely carry tree ferns of appreciable size. No doubt you have seen a small Mexican tree fern and mistaken it for an ordinary fern. But if you shop around, you should be able to find specimens with rough brown shaggy trunks from two to five feet tall. These are genuine, mature tree ferns, and they are really spectacular-looking indoor trees.

Tree ferns, like ferns in general, will dry up and disintegrate in hot, direct sunlight. On the other hand, they also don't like heavy shade. The ideal solution is to give them gentle, filtered light. We keep our Mexican tree fern in our dining room, which gets filtered sunlight from windows facing north and west. Several hedges and tall trees outdoors shield the room from scorching light. In the summer it is the coolest room in the house. Still, the walls are painted white, and on sunny days the room is bright enough to read and write in without turning on the lights. It is an ideal room in which to grow ferns. All our ferns, dangling in paint buckets and cans from hooks in the window frames, do beautifully there.

Watering a tree fern is not especially difficult, so long as you use tepid water and *always* keep the soil moist to the touch but never soupy or soggy. You will definitely need to get a tree fern sitter to water the plant when you're away on trips. Since all tree ferns grow in jungle climates, they thrive on high humidity. The Mexican tree fern tolerates dry air better than all the other species combined, but it still appreciates a daily misting in the winter and does best when set near other plants. Keeping a humidifier going in the room in winter certainly won't hurt.

Tree ferns can be grown exclusively in water. The trunk must be propped up with stones or rocks, but they will grow as well in water as in soil.

If you buy a *Cyathea arborea,* or West Indian tree fern, you should keep its trunk constantly moist. It also requires humid, circulating air. Our advice is to avoid this species unless you own a greenhouse.

Feed your tree fern only once every six months and then use a water-soluble plant food diluted to half the recommended strength. Wait six months before you feed a newly purchased tree.

When repotting, use ordinary commercial potting soil.

Except for the *Dicksonia squarrosa,* which needs cool air in the fifties and low sixties at night, all the other tree ferns prefer warm, humid air. Avoid exposing them to radical shifts in temperature. Keep in a reasonably warm room, preferably above 55 degrees.

Tree Philodendron
(Philodendron selloum)

This extremely hardy plant from the jungles of Brazil should give you more pleasure and less trouble than almost any tree in this book. It is famous for its large, tough, shiny, dark green, deeply lobed leaves. The tree philodendron grows fast, adapts to either light or shade, seldom needs water, and is virtually pest-free. In the summer, it is fascinating to watch its fresh new leaves unfurl.

Tree philodendron (*Philodendron selloum*).

We have seen a tree philodendron at the Botanic Gardens in Washington, D.C., with a trunk six feet tall, six inches thick, and leaves three feet across. The trunk looked like a segment of a python, its diamond-patterned beige-brown bark like python skin. But this was a real monster, and most tree philodendrons in plant stores do not have trunks.

Philodendrons are epiphytic jungle plants, or "air plants," which means that in their native habitat they rely on other trees for support, and receive most of their water and nourishment from the air. The word "philodendron" means "tree-loving" in Greek. This should give you some idea of what the plants like best: high humidity, heat, and shade.

But the tree philodendron is so tough that we keep one of ours in the shade, another in a moderate amount of light, and a third one near a window facing east. All three do equally well. The only thing the plants won't tolerate is strong, direct sunlight in the summer, or they will wilt and their leaves will scorch.

The tree philodendron is so tough that it can go a month or longer without water and survive. But it should normally be watered when the top of its soil dries out. We feed ours every three weeks in the summer with a water-soluble fertilizer or Plant Tabs. In the winter, we cut the fertilizing back to every six weeks or two months.

The tree philodendron looks its best if you plant two or three of them together in a tub or a large pot. The effect is fuller, lusher, and more striking than one plant growing alone.

As for the long, trailing air roots on these plants, you can either cut them off or keep them on. It makes no difference to the plant, since it is getting most of its water from the soil now, not the air. Still, many plant books and plant shop owners insist that you must leave the air roots on. We once saw a large tree philodendron in a plant shop with its air roots snaking all over the floor. At the end of each root was a battered little Dixie cup filled with water. The owner was sure the plant would suffer if its roots didn't get their daily drink. To settle the question, we visited a philodendron grower last year in central Florida. When we put the question to him, he just laughed. "Sure you can cut the air roots off," he said. "Who wants air roots all over the house?"

The tree can be propagated by cutting off a stem and potting it in moist potting soil. You can also grow it from seed in a small pot filled with moist potting soil, covering the pot with plastic wrap. The only place we have been able to find the seeds is Park Seed Co., Inc., Greenwood, S.C. 29647. They also carry seeds for the magnificent *Monstera deliciosa,* or "Swiss cheese philodendron," which also grows to tree size and requires the same care as the tree philodendron.

Yew Pine or Buddhist Pine
(Podocarpus macrophyllus)

For a dramatic illustration of how slow-growing the yew pine is, examine the photograph on page 17 comparing its rate of growth to a schefflera's. While both trees were started from seed at the same time, the schefflera grew five feet in a year and

Yew pine (*Podocarpus macrophyllus*).

Broadleaf podocarpus (*Podocarpus nagi*).

a half, but the yew pine grew only eight inches! If you want a tree-size yew pine, we suggest you buy one full-grown.

The yew pine has soft, bright green, needle-like leaves one to three inches long and grows to sixty feet outdoors in its native China and Japan. Indoor specimens above five feet are hard to find. Nicely sculpted standards such as the one pictured are definitely not the norm. This is one indoor tree that really benefits from pruning. The tree pictured did not accidentally acquire its full shape; it was carefully pruned and trimmed from an early age to look that way. For best results, prune your yew pine in early spring before the tree develops new growth—it will spring back like a hedge if you do.

While the yew pine is one of the most truly tree-like and non-tropical-looking of indoor trees, it can be tricky to grow. Since it lives in subtropical regions, it needs cool night air to thrive. Ideally, it should get night temperatures between 40 and 55 degrees in winter. Since this requirement may be difficult to provide, at least try to keep the tree in the coolest location in your home. Be especially careful not to keep it near a hot air duct or a radiator. A cool glassed-in sun porch where the temperature does not drop below 40 degrees is an ideal location for the tree. In summer, consider moving it outdoors if you have a porch or patio. No doubt some yew pines will survive under stuffier conditions, but as a general rule they prefer cool air and good air circulation.

The tree also likes direct sunlight, bright filtered light, or bright indirect light reflected off a light wall. Do not place it in a dim corner, unless you can provide it with strong artificial lighting for at least twelve hours a day.

Water the yew pine moderately with tepid water. The top of the soil, but no deeper, should be powder-dry before you water it. As with all your plants and trees, give it enough water to soak the entire pot. Then let the water drain out the drainage hole and empty the dish in which it stands. The best test to see if the soil is dry or moist is to stick your finger all the way down into the soil. Obviously, you should water the tree if the soil feels dry, but refrain from watering it if it still feels moist.

A variety of the yew pine is the *Podocarpus macrophyllus maki,* or southern yew, which has shorter needles and is more shrub-like than the common yew pine. Perhaps the loveliest podocarpus of all is the *P. nagi* with small, shiny, dark green, pointed leaves. Both these trees should be cared for the same way as the yew pine, although the *nagi* prefers a more arid soil. *P. gracilior,* or fern pine, has gray-green needles and is also available in many plant stores.

All these trees can be fertilized once a month in spring and summer when young, but they need to be fed only twice a year if already specimen size. Propagation is by stem cutting.

Yucca Tree

(including *Yucca brevifolia, Y. elephantipes,* and *Y. marginata*)

These slow-growing but potentially enormous trees are ideal to grow indoors. They require little care and are almost as durable as a rubber tree or a corn plant. All they need is bright light and fairly dry soil. If you treat them as you would a cactus or a succulent, you can't go wrong.

Yuccas are one of the few groups of hardy indoor trees that are really native to America. The Joshua tree (*Y. brevifolia*) ranges from California to Utah and has an amazing, grotesquely branching trunk which sometimes grows forty feet tall. You have no doubt seen this unusual desert tree lurking in the background of cowboy movies. The spineless yucca or *Y. elephantipes* is native to Mexico and Guatemala and has an erect trunk with rough brown bark and a swollen base. Both of these trees, as well as the *Yucca marginata,* have essentially the same long, green, bayonet-shaped leaves. The *marginata,* however, has creamy-white edges on its leaves.

The trees are closely related to the common yucca plants one sees growing in yards and along highways in the South. They all produce white, waxy flowers, indoors as well as out, which appear in the spring on erect shoots growing from the center of the leaves.

The ingredients for growing yucca trees successfully indoors are simple—plenty of sunshine, a well-drained soil, and only a moderate amount of water (otherwise the roots and even the trunk will start to rot).

When watering, always allow the top of the soil to become powder-dry. It is imperative not to water a yucca tree if the soil looks dark on top and still feels moist.

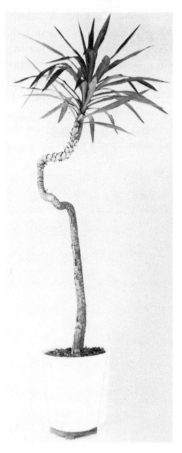

Joshua tree (*Yucca brevifolia*).
(Photo by Everet Conklin
Companies, International)

Think of them as desert trees which are accustomed to sudden, heavy rains followed by weeks and months of endless drought. For large trees in containers twelve inches in diameter or larger, let the top two inches of the soil dry out. For plants in smaller pots, wait until you can scratch up enough dry surface soil to sift through your hand. The trees will need even less water in the winter. But don't be miserly when you get around to watering them. Soak the pot so that all the soil gets moist, then empty the drainage dish in which it stands.

Yucca trees will grow best in direct sunlight at any exposure, but they will do almost as well in bright indirect or filtered light. Avoid placing them in heavy shade for very long.

The trees are slow-growing and cannot absorb excess amounts of food. Feed young plants with a water-soluble fertilizer every two or three months. Mature specimens should be fed only twice a year.

In spring and summer, you may want to move your tree outdoors. The wind, rain, and fresh air will make it grow more vigorously, but take precautions to protect it from the harsh rays of the sun the first few days. Give it a chance to get acclimatized to the hot sun by keeping it at first in the shade. By remembering to rotate your tree every so often you will be able to maintain a symmetrical trunk.

Although the demands this tree makes for humidity are relatively small, the leaves do tend to droop if the air becomes excessively dry. They can be revived by syringing with tepid water. As with most foliage plants, the yucca's leaves should be kept free from dust by wiping with a clean damp cloth. This also helps eliminate the possibilities of pests. If your tree is bothered by mealy bugs or scale, treat with Malathion. Red spider mites usually succumb to Kelthane.

Yuccas will need repotting only every four or five years. Use ordinary commercial potting soil mixed with rough sand, and step up the size of the pot by one or two inches if the tree has outgrown its old pot—or trim its roots (see page 24) and replant in the same pot.

All three of these trees will grow well in normal house temperatures, but they aren't bothered by drafts and they may grow even better with cool night temperatures in the winter. Never expose them to frost or temperatures much below 40 degrees.

Appendix

List of Plants by Botanical Name

BOTANICAL NAME	COMMON NAME
Araucaria araucana	Monkey-puzzle tree
A. bidwillii	Monkey-puzzle tree
A. excelsa	Norfolk Island pine
Ardisia crispa	Coral berry
Beaucarnea recurvata	Ponytail palm
	Elephant-foot tree
Brassaia actinophylla	Schefflera
	Umbrella tree
Caryota mitis	Fishtail palm
Chamaedorea elegans	Parlor palm
C. erumpens	Bamboo palm
Chamaerops humilis	European fan palm
Chrysalidocarpus lutescens	Areca palm
Cibotium chamissoi	Hawaiian tree fern
C. schiedei	Mexican tree fern
Citrus mitis	Panama orange tree
C. paradisi	Grapefruit tree
C. ponderosa	Lemon tree
C. taitensis	Otaheite orange tree
Clusia rosea	Autograph tree
Coccoloba uvifera	Sea grape
Codiaeum variegatum	Croton
Coffea arabica	Coffee tree
Cordyline terminalis	Hawaiian ti
Crassula argentea	Jade tree
Cyathea arborea	West Indian tree fern
Cycas revoluta	Sago palm
	Pineapple palm
Dieffenbachia amoena	Giant dumb cane
Dizygotheca elegantissima	False aralia
Dracaena deremensis 'Janet Craig'	Dragon tree
D. deremensis warneckei	
D. draco	
D. fragrans	Corn plant
D. fragrans massangeana	Corn plant
D. hookeriana	
D. marginata	

BOTANICAL NAME	COMMON NAME
Eriobotrya japonica	Loquat tree
	Japanese plum
Eucalyptus cinera	Silver dollar eucalyptus
E. citriodora	Lemon eucalyptus
E. globulus	Tasmanian blue gum
Euphorbia lactea	Candelabra cactus
E. pulcherrima	Poinsettia
E. tirucallii	Pencil cactus
Fatsia japonica	Japanese aralia
Ficus benghalensis	Banyan tree
F. benjamina	Weeping fig
F. carica	Common fig tree
F. diversifolia	Mistletoe fig
F. elastica	Rubber tree
F. lyrata	Fiddle-leaf fig
F. religiosa	Bo tree
F. retusa nitida	Indian laurel
F. rubiginosa	Rusty fig
F. triangularis	Triangle-leafed fig
Grevillea robusta	Silk oak
Howea forsteriana	Kentia palm
Jasminum grandiflorum	Jasmine
Ligustrum lucidum	Privet
Livistona chinensis	Chinese fan palm
Musa cavendishii	Chinese dwarf banana
M. nana	Dwarf banana
Pandanus utilis	Screw pine
Persa americana	Avocado tree
	Alligator pear
Philodendron selloum	Tree philodendron
Phoenix roebelenii	Pygmy date palm
Pittosporum tobira	Japanese pittosporum
	Australian laurel
Pleomele reflexa	Yew pine
Podocarpus macrophyllus	Buddhist pine
Polyscias balfouriana	Balfour aralia
P. fruticosa	Ming tree
Rhapis excelsa	Lady palm
Solanum pseudo-capsicum	Jerusalem cherry tree
Yucca brevifolia	Joshua tree
Y. elephantipes	Yucca tree
Y. marginata	Yucca tree

Where to Find Indoor Trees

It would be impossible to list in detail the increasing number of tropical plant stores and nurseries which carry indoor trees. There are literally thousands of them, many unbelievably well stocked, in cities, suburbs, and outlying towns. Suburban garden centers are often the best place to look for hard-to-find species. Why? Perhaps because they have been in the business longer, know their plants better, and have more space. Also perhaps because suburban homes tend to have more light and space than city apartments and can accommodate a wider range of indoor trees. And don't forget about the garden section of many discount stores. Bargains on indoor trees can sometimes be found there.

If you are having trouble locating a particular kind of indoor tree, first ask your local plant store if they can order it for you. If not, consult the list below for the supplier nearest you.

Everet Conklin Companies, International
7 Brook Avenue
Montvale, New Jersey 07645

Specialists in plant rental; wide variety of indoor trees.

Florida Cactus, Inc.
General Delivery
Apopka, Florida 32703

Spectacular selection of cactuses and succulents, large and small.

George W. Park Seed Co., Inc.
P. O. Box 31
Greenwood, South Carolina 29647

Dependable supplier of seeds for indoor trees; write for catalogue.

Interior Plant Distributors
12241 Nebel Street
Rockville, Maryland 20852

Retail outlet with one of the largest supplies of indoor trees in the District of Columbia area.

John's Inc. "Dewkist" Nurseries
P. O. Drawer AC
Apopka, Florida 32703

Large wholesale dealer in indoor trees and smaller plants; good place to inquire about hard-to-find species.

Julius Roehrs Co.
Route 33
Farmingdale, New Jersey 07727

Fine selection of indoor trees; no mail order.

Lexington Gardens
93 Hancock Street
Lexington, Massachusetts 02173

Good place to look in Boston area for indoor trees.

Nielsen's Greenhouses
1405 Post Road
Darien, Connecticut 06820

Exceptionally large stock of indoor trees; high-priced but worth a look; inquire about mail order.

Plants 'N Things
6318 Peters Creek Road
Hollins, Virginia 24019

Retail outlet for plants and indoor trees up to six feet; wide range of species.

Seminole Nurseries
7800 Seminole Blvd.
Seminole, Florida 33542

Bonsai specialists; inquire about mail order.

Terrestris
409 East 60th Street
New York, N.Y. 10022

Large supplier of indoor trees; specimens up to twenty feet; write for catalogue.

Wildwood Gardens
Box 296
North Conway, New Hampshire 03860

Excellent source of indoor trees and smaller plants; will answer mail order inquiries.

Bibliography

Abraham, George, *The Green Thumb Book of Indoor Gardening; A Complete Guide.* Prentice-Hall, 1967.

Bailey, L. H., *How Plants Get Their Names.* The Macmillan Company, 1933.

Beatty, Virginia, *Consumer Guide's Rating and Raising Indoor Plants.* Publications International, Ltd., 1975.

Chidamian, Claude, *Bonsai—Miniature Trees.* D. Van Nostrand Co., 1955.

————, *The Book of Cacti and Other Succulents.* Doubleday & Company, Inc., 1958.

Crockett, James Underwood, *Foliage House Plants.* Time-Life Books, 1972.

Evans, Charles M., and Pliner, Roberta Lee, *RX for Ailing House Plants.* Random House, 1974.

Foliage Plants for Modern Living. Merchants Publishing Company, 1974.

The Garden Dictionary. Houghton Mifflin Company, 1938.

Graf, Alfred Byrd, *Exotic House Plants.* Roehrs Company, 1973.

————, *Exotica 3.* Roehrs Company, 1970.

Johnson, Hugh, *International Book of Trees.* Simon & Schuster, 1973.

Hull, George F., *Bonsai for Americans.* Doubleday & Company, Inc., 1964.

Kromdijk, G., *200 House Plants in Color.* Lutterworth Press, 1967.

Langer, Richard W., *The After-Dinner Gardening Book.* Collier Books, 1969.

Perper, Hazel, *The Avocado Pit Grower's Indoor How-to Book.* Walker and Company, 1965.

Staff of the L. H. Bailey Hortorium, Cornell University, *Hortus Third: A Dictionary of Plants Cultivated in the United States and Canada.* Macmillan, 1976.

Taloumis, George, *House Plants for Five Exposures.* The New American Library, Inc., 1973.

Terrestris, *Indoor Plant Selection and Survival Guide.* Grosset & Dunlap, 1973.

Index